COOKING WITH
JENNY MORRIS

SUNBIRD PUBLISHERS

SUNBIRD PUBLISHERS

First published in 2011

Sunbird Publishers (Pty) Ltd
The illustrated imprint of
Jonathan Ball Publishers
P O Box 6836
Roggebaai 8012
Cape Town, South Africa
www.sunbirdpublishers.co.za

Registration number: 1984/003543/07

www.jennymorris.co.za
www.gigglinggourmet.com

The following trademarks are the
property of the author: Jenny Morris®,
Giggling Gourmet®, CooksPlayground™,
TeamCooking™, CooksParty™,
CooksCourse™, UCooking™ and
FrequentFryer™

Design and typesetting by MR Design
Cover design by MR Design
Editing and project management by Michelle Marlin
Proofreading by Kathleen Sutton
Photographs by Danie Nel Photography
Photographs on pages 20, 106, 124, 226, 256, 260, 266 © iStock
Food styling by Abigail Donnelly
Food assistant, Hannah Lewry
Printed and bound by Star Standard Industries (Pte) Ltd
(Singapore)

ISBN 978-1-920289-38-6

Thank you

This book is dedicated with love to my husband David. Thank you for all your unconditional love and support!

I have so many special people in my life and without their mouths to feed it would have taken forever to test my recipes. Even though they were not aware that they were being used as guinea pigs, they all deserve a big fat kiss – it is because of them that it was easy to choose what to keep and what to ditch! My special thanks go to my most honest and tireless critics, Jeff and Myrna Wittels, who must have ploughed their way through at least 200 dishes.

I just couldn't have done this without my staff at the Cook's Playground. To my sweet Marga Swart, who has managed to decipher the recipes written in my sleep, thank you for your dedication and the back-breaking hours you spent at the keyboard. Abdul Isaacs, you are a Super Being; thank you for all you do for me! To our new friend for life, Steven Schmitt, we have loved having you at the Cook's Playground; thank you for being part of my team. Carolize Odendaal, our student chef from 'The Culinary Academy', you worked like a little demon on the food shoots. And a huge thank you to Patricia Nokela, who washed up hundreds of pots, pans and bowls while we were shooting the book; she was richly rewarded with 'takeaways'.

A great big thank you to the team who put this book together. To my publisher Ceri Prenter, I do not have words. Thank you for your vision; may we sail along together for many more publications. Abigail Donnelly, my soul sister when it comes to food, you understand that a soft egg needs to 'tremble'! Michelle Marlin, you got straight into my head and understand my hungry soul. Marius Roux, thank you for being my wonderful 'design man'. Special thanks to Danie Nel; I love your work darling one!

Many thanks to Jack Wittles from Zanddrift Farm for delivering the best pomegranates I have ever seen in my life right on time for my photo shoot!

And to God ...I thank you for everything.

Contents

Foreword

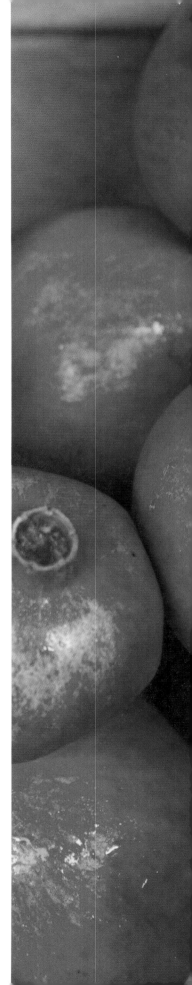

I felt very privileged to be asked to write the foreword to Jenny's third book, *Cooking with Jenny Morris*.

I have known Jenny from early on in her culinary career, when I first asked her to take part in the Good Food and Wine Show. Jenny wowed visitors to the show with her passion for good food, her sense of humour and her imaginative, accessible cooking style.

At the time Jenny was a radio presenter on 567 Cape Talk (and still is) hosting the weekly food feature. More recently she has caught the eye of Food Network and presents their first commissioned television show in South Africa. As an author, teacher and brand ambassador for 'new' South African cuisine, she has travelled the world, inspired by people, places and unusual ingredients.

Combining her wealth of experience and boundless creative energy, Jenny has compiled a treasury of recipes that pays tribute to her passion for good quality, fresh ingredients and her enthusiasm for interesting flavours.

Jenny, also known as the Giggling Gourmet, lives her brand. Her laughter resonates; from her eclectic family home to every demonstration or celebrity appearance she makes. She is comfortable demonstrating alongside the world's leading celebrity chefs, or sitting in a small brightly lit Chinese takeaway shop, enjoying a freshly caught fish, sweet and sour.

Jenny has an intuition for good food and is able to share her passion with every mouthful. She believes in tasting as you go along, provocatively of course. Beneath Jenny's sexy love affair with food, is a unique individual, with a heart larger than her kitchen ... a mother who loves to feed her children the best of life in all its guises, a sexy wife that most men can only dream of, a very special friend, and a mentor to the youth entering this exciting industry.

Jen, I am so proud of you. Keep cooking, laughing and sharing your unique interpretations of global flavours.

Christine Cashmore
Director of the Good Food and Wine Show ®

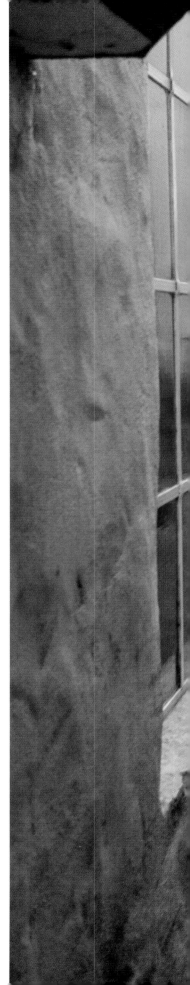

Welcome to the
Cook's Playground

There is a little alleyway in the heart of De Waterkant that leads to one of my favourite places. As you walk along the cobbles, you might hear the clattering of pots and pans, or the whirr of a blender. Passing an open window, you will be enveloped by the most intoxicating aromas; bread baking in the oven, spices tempered in a pan, or something garlicky bubbling away on the stove.

When you get to the end of the alley, open the door – go on, don't be shy! And there you are; at the Cook's Playground, the place where all my dreams as a chef have come true.

It must be nearly nine years ago now that David and I decided that we needed a dedicated kitchen from which to run our catering business and a permanent home for my growing culinary school. The building we were in at the time was being redeveloped and during the finishing stages of the revamp, I noticed an alleyway across the street. As I walked down that little alley, I just knew that I had found the perfect spot.

Since then the Cook's Playground has played host to countless feasts and foodie events. I especially enjoy our corporate Team Cooking evenings (or lunchtimes) and our Cook's Parties for celebrating special occasions. Nothing excites me more than seeing how a bunch of raw, nervous recruits, who all claim that they can't cook, end up making the most spectacular meals. I just love to watch their faces when they tuck in to the food that they have made by themselves from scratch!

Although most of my experiments and recipe development happens in my own kitchen at home, it is at the Cook's Playground that they are put through their paces. It is here that the recipes are tested and tasted and finally come into their own.

I love to cook and I love to share my joy in food with others, and with the Cook's Playground I have had so many opportunities to do exactly that. But where did it all begin? If I think about it, my journey as a cook started many years ago in the gardens of my childhood.

I was lucky enough to have parents and grandparents who were passionate about growing the most spectacular fruit and veggies imaginable, and using them to prepare honest, hearty meals.

I think that is why I am still so crazy about anything that is fresh. All those simple, beautiful tastes and flavours from my childhood are forever stored in my memory bank. Like the gorgeous omelettes turned into a feast just by stirring chopped herbs into the beaten eggs. And the jewelled babies from the uterus of the glorious pomegranates that grew on the edible windbreaks my grandfather built, because he believed that even something functional could be a source of food. Even the petals from my grandmother's pride and joy, her rose garden, could be sugared and used to decorate a luscious, home-baked cake.

When I was growing up, a carrot from our garden tasted like a carrot! You just can't beat those flavours. I urge everyone to try to grow something just to experience that wonderful taste of freshness. You don't need a lot of space; you can even grow carrots in a coffee tin, and tomatoes in a bag of soil.

Growing up surrounded by all this led quite naturally to my great interest in food. My dream, quite simply, was to feed other people. I always wanted to be a chef but my father didn't let me live my dream. I get quite angry when I think back on it now and my advice is that if you want a career in food you should never let anyone hold you back.

This was the man who taught me so much about food – how to grow it, how to harvest it, how to catch it, how to cook it, how to eat it – and yet he deprived me of my passion! All I wanted was to surround myself with food and the chance to feed others. I could never understand it at the time, but his reasoning was that he didn't want me sweating over pots in a kitchen full of men. 'One day you are going to get married and have babies, so forget about that nonsense,' he said. 'Just grow your own food and cook it for your family.'

Of course, I have done that and more besides, but I got my own back on him and, in an act of defiance, became telephone technician and worked in the Post Office. And you know what? I'd go back and do it all again.

But if you have a passion for food, never give up on it even if there isn't money for a formal education or training. Go to a restaurant or a hotel, even if you have to start by washing dishes and work your way up. My former gardener Isaac works in my kitchen now and he rolls a spring roll better than any Chinaman.

When I think about a recipe, I see it as an idea, as a combination of flavours that could live happily together. I believe anyone can put a recipe together. When you're out shopping and see wonderful fresh ingredients, look at them and ask yourself what you can do with them. Anyone can cook a meal that you could fall in love with.

Don't be intimidated by the pictures you see in recipe books. Many of my friends say that they can't cook, because their efforts never look like those wonderful photographs. But that is not what cooking is all about – you need to realise that your tastes are personal and that they belong to you. You don't have to try to make something that looks or tastes exactly the same as a dish you just had at your best friend's house, or at a restaurant. Instead, use those meals as an inspiration, and make your creations your own.

You have to trust yourself and be adventurous, so get in your kitchen now and start to play! We all have these wonderful senses of touch, sound, smell and taste. Food is not just about eating, and you should learn to trust your instincts and your senses. People say, 'I don't know when it's ready'. Well, I love listening to my food cooking, because it sizzles, pops, hisses and bubbles, letting me know when it is done. You can smell when food changes, when it's time to turn it over, when it lets go in the pan. Trust yourself.

Every good dish starts off with something that is fabulously fresh. The best thing that's ever going to happen to me in my life is to cook with the simplest, freshest ingredients. Let them excite you the way they do me. I layer my flavours and, as the dish takes shape, I taste as I go along. Don't over-complicate things and don't put flavours in there that don't happily co-exist – you wouldn't invite people to a dinner party who don't get along, would you?

I take people on food tours around the world because I want them to experience what I do. I say that food makes you feel passionate, whether you like to cook it, shop for it, eat it, dream about it, look at it, read about it, or touch it. I do all these things and if you enjoy them as well, then I want to be in your company.

Welcome to the Cook's Playground – let's start cooking!

CHAPTER ONE

Rise and *Shine*

My grandpa Bob Cannon made crumpets every single day of the week – this he did without fail. They were gorgeous, light and fluffy; caramelised on the outside and soft and spongy on the inside. I would wait for the call, 'Sookie put your shoes on, it's tea time,' and with that I would gallop down the path and through the gate over to their side of the property and have tea with my grandparents in their huge house.

Believe it or not, I wasn't really crazy about the crumpets themselves. What I loved was licking off the delicious blobs of salty butter he would put on them (and anyone who knows me knows I cannot live without lots of butter!) which would melt and mingle with the runny honey. I think that I ate only one of those crumpets but licked five others clean.

I was very lucky to have a grandfather who made me crumpets.

Become a smooth operator

I am sure that my mother invented smoothies. When we were kids, she used to put anything in milk along with a raw egg because it was good for us. My sister Beverley and I would kick up our heels at this. Raw egg! Yuk! How on earth could it be good for you? So she used to mash a banana into it with some honey and a little cinnamon, and that went down a treat; better than the weekly cod liver oil and orange juice we used to get!

Now I can't wait to fling a bunch of fruit or veggies into my smoothie maker, and add some nuts and honey, and even a raw egg from time to time. It's just a wonderful way to get a glassful of nutrition to start you off for the day.

Bangkok smoothie

- 1 can litchis, strained and syrup reserved
- 250 ml coconut milk
- ½ cup honey or palm sugar
- 2 stems lemon grass, soft white part bruised and chopped
- zest and juice of 2 fresh limes
- 1 cup Greek yoghurt
- 2 teaspoons grated fresh ginger
- fresh mint, for garnishing

Place the syrup from the litchis in a saucepan with the coconut milk, honey, bruised lemon grass and lime zest. Heat gently and when it starts to simmer, remove from the heat and let the lemon grass infuse in the coconut milk.

Place the cooled, strained coconut milk in a blender with the litchis, lime juice, yoghurt and fresh ginger. Add a few blocks of ice and blend till smooth. Serve ice cold garnished with fresh lime and mint.

SERVES 4

TIP: This is delicious made with fresh litchis; use a cup of pitted fresh ones and a cup of litchi juice.

Pawpaw shake

- 2 tablespoons runny honey
- 150 g ripe pawpaw, peeled and cubed
- ½ cup coconut milk
- 2 teaspoons chopped fresh ginger
- 1 cup cold low fat milk
- ice cubes
- zest and juice of 1 lime

Blitz all the ingredients together in a blender, and pour into tall chilled glasses.

SERVES 2

"Once a woman has forgiven her man, she must not reheat his sins for breakfast."

Marlene Dietrich

Energy in a glass

- ½ spanspek melon
- 1 ripe mango or large cling peach, chopped
- 1 tablespoon honey
- 2 tablespoons muesli
- zest of 1 orange
- 1 orange, juiced
- ½ cup peach or apricot yoghurt
- 250 ml low fat milk
- 1 tablespoon Horlicks

Peel the melon, seed it and chop roughly. Blend the fruit, honey and muesli in a blender till smooth. Add the remaining ingredients, and blend till creamy and foaming. Pour into chilled glasses.

SERVES 4

Melon and ginger breakfast boost

- 1 kg watermelon chunks, without seeds
- 1 cup fresh pineapple, chopped
- 3–5 cm fresh ginger, peeled and roughly chopped
- ½ cup fresh mint
- 1 ½ cups pomegranate juice
- honey to taste

Place all the ingredients in a blender and whizz till smooth. Pour into a large glass jug and serve chilled, topped with crushed ice.

SERVES 6

Sundried apricot, prune and ginger standby

I like to keep this in the fridge and have a few spoonfuls with natural yoghurt for breakfast. It is also delicious warmed up and served with a dollop of mascarpone cheese as a standby dessert.

- 2 ½ cups sparkling apple juice
- 1 cup sugar
- peel of 1 lemon (no pith)
- 50 g peeled ginger, cut into matchsticks
- seeds of 2 green cardamom pods
- 30 pitted prunes
- 30 plump sundried apricots

Place the apple juice, sugar, lemon peel, ginger and cardamom seeds in a saucepan and bring to the boil slowly, stirring all the time to dissolve the sugar. Simmer gently for 10 minutes. Then add the prunes and apricots and cook slowly till the fruit is swollen. Add a little more apple juice if need be.

Let the fruit cool in the syrup and then transfer to the fridge till you need it. When I say transfer I mean everything – lemon peel, ginger, the lot – let all the flavours fuse into one another.

If you find this a little too sweet, add some freshly-squeezed lemon juice to round it off.

SERVES 4

Breakfast-heaven on a plate, especially if you can get your hands on some little red and ripe strawberries that come straight from the plant; okay maybe a day or so old!

When we were children, we would go out into the garden and pick plump and juicy strawberries, hot and fragrant from the sun.

Fresh strawberry crêpes

THE CRÊPES
- 125 g cake flour
- pinch of salt
- 2 eggs
- 120 ml low fat milk
- 120 ml water
- 30 g butter, melted

THE FILLING
- 3 tablespoons icing sugar
- 2 cups chopped seasonal strawberries
- 250 ml mascarpone

You need to place the flour, salt and eggs in a large mixing bowl and whisk them together well. Now, gradually whisk in the milk and water, stirring all the time to combine. Add the butter and beat it until it is smooth.

Heat a non-stick frying pan and oil it lightly. Pour about a ¼ cup of batter into the pan and keep tilting it to swirl the batter so that it covers the surface of the pan in a thin, even layer. Cook each crêpe for about 2 minutes, or until the bottom is light brown. Gently loosen the crêpe with a spatula, flip it over and cook the other side. Stack onto a plate and serve with the filling.

To make the filling, sprinkle the icing sugar over the strawberries and fold the berries into the mascarpone.

Place the crêpes onto a flat surface and fill with the strawberry cream. Roll into a cigar shape, cut in half and arrange on a white plate. Dust with icing sugar and garnish with a few fresh strawberries.

You can fill the crêpes with anything that takes your fancy; I love juicy plump figs with Brie and bacon, and blueberries and, and ... oh darlings, fill it with whatever makes your mouth love you!

SERVES 4

TIP: Don't keep strawberries for longer than 2 days in the fridge and do not wash them until you are ready to use them; only then do you wash them and remove the stems.

Jenny's muffins

These muffins were a favourite at the cake counter of my coffee shop – visitors used to buy takeaways for later. We used to make them all day to keep up. The muffins freeze beautifully, so don't be shy to bake a big batch.

THE MUFFINS
- 4 eggs, beaten
- 2 cups brown sugar
- 1 ½ cups vegetable oil
- 1 ½ cups buttermilk
- 3 cups cake flour, sifted
- 2 teaspoons ground cinnamon
- 2 teaspoons baking powder
- 2 teaspoons bicarb
- ½ teaspoon salt
- 1 cup chopped, mixed glacé fruit
- 3 tablespoons poppy seeds
- ½ cup roughly chopped sultanas
- ½ cup chopped pecan nuts (optional)
- ½ cup desiccated coconut (optional)

THE TOPPING
- 2 teaspoons ground cinnamon
- 6 tablespoons brown sugar
- ½ cup sunflower seeds

Mix the eggs, sugar, oil and buttermilk together. Then place all the dry ingredients in a large mixing bowl.

Combine the glacé fruit, poppy seeds, sultanas, nuts and coconut (if using) and add them to the dry mix, stirring together thoroughly to coat the fruit with flour. Make a well in the centre of the flour and stir in the buttermilk mixture. Do not over-mix!

Spoon into a greased muffin tin; don't over-fill. Now mix the cinnamon and brown sugar together and sprinkle over the muffins, and then sprinkle the sunflower seeds over the top. (My children used to steal this topping off all the muffins!)

Bake for 15 to 20 minutes, or until a skewer or toothpick inserted into the centre of the muffin comes out clean. Take the muffins out of the oven and leave in the tin for 5 minutes before removing them to cool on a wire rack.

These muffins are delicious with lots of cold butter and a slice of mature cheddar cheese or a dollop of Fairview Chevin!

MAKES 18

Ripen your bananas quickly by placing them in a paper bag with an apple or a tomato. Close the bag and let the ethylene gas released by the fruit ripen them in next to no time. Let the garden have the peels once you are done!

Banana pancakes topped with bacon, Brie and caramelised pear

THE TOPPING

- 8 rashers streaky bacon or pancetta
- a knob of butter
- 2 firm pears, sliced
- honey to drizzle
- 8 slices ripe Brie cheese

THE PANCAKES

- 2 ripe bananas, peeled and well mashed
- 2 eggs
- 2 teaspoons castor sugar
- 30 g melted butter
- 1 teaspoon vanilla extract
- 1 ½ cups self-raising flour
- ½ teaspoon bicarbonate of soda

Fry the bacon till nice and crispy. Remove from the pan and drain on a paper towel. Add the butter to the same pan and lightly fry the pear slices on both sides. Drizzle with honey while still in the pan and set aside while you make the pancakes.

Place all the ingredients for the pancake batter in a blender and blend till smooth. Heat a non-stick frying pan over medium heat and grease lightly with a little butter.

Place about 2 tablespoons of batter into the pan and smooth out, cook for about 2 minutes or until bubbles start to appear on the surface. Turn and cook the other side till nice and golden. Remove from the pan and keep warm while you make pancakes with the remaining batter.

Arrange some pears, Brie and bacon on each pancake, and serve with a bowl of sprouts on the side.

SERVES 4

TIP: If you don't eat pork, top with macon or chicken bacon. These pancakes are just as good topped with some butter and honey and sliced banana.

Did you know?

Bananas are rich in potassium, which makes you feel sexy and alert, and in vitamin B, which is a good one for taking the edge off the nerves! The fibre in bananas not only keeps digestion regular, but also helps maintain blood sugar levels and curbs overeating.

These delicious cold omelettes also make a wonderful starter or can be served as quaint snacks for a drinks party.

Herbed omelettes filled with smoked salmon and cucumber

THE OMELETTES
- 5 eggs
- ¼ cup finely chopped fresh coriander, mint, dill and parsley (with stalks)
- pinch of salt
- coarse black pepper
- sunflower oil or olive oil for frying

THE FILLING
- 200 g smoked salmon
- ½ an English cucumber
- 60 ml mayonnaise
- 1 teaspoon chopped dill
- 1 spring onion with tops, finely chopped
- 1 teaspoon lemon juice
- freshly ground black pepper
- finely grated zest of 1 small ripe lemon

Whisk the eggs in a bowl and add the chopped herbs. Add a pinch of salt and freshly ground black pepper.

Heat a 20 cm frying pan till smoking hot, add 1 ml sunflower oil and turn the heat halfway down. Pour 35 ml of the egg and herb mixture into the pan and coat evenly. As soon as the egg mixture is cooked, loosen the sides and remove from the pan with a plastic spatula.

Place the pancake cooked-side down on baking paper and cool.

To make the filling, cut the salmon into ribbons 2.5 cm wide and divide into 6 portions. Trim the edges of the cucumber, quarter it and remove the seeds. Cut into batons 5 cm long and 3 mm thick. Mix the mayonnaise with the rest of the ingredients in a small bowl, and place in the fridge till needed.

When all the omelettes are cooked, put it all together. Coat each omelette with 7.5 ml of the mayonnaise mixture ensuring that the sides are covered as well (this will seal the omelette when rolled). Place the sliced salmon 1 cm away from the edge and top with two pieces of cucumber placed next to one another. Flip the pancake edge over the mixture and then roll tightly into the shape of a cigar.

Garnish with a sprig of coriander or dill and some fresh mint, and enjoy!

MAKES 6

D̲on't you love it when you slice through the middle of a ripe pumpkin and the sticky beads of juice start forming, and all those beautiful pips surrounded by edible pumpkin hairs are exposed and the perfume hits you? I just want to look at it all day.

Pumpkin fritters

Serve these fritters for breakfast with lots of runny honey and thick, creamy Greek yoghurt. Keep the pumpkin seeds and wash and dry them. Roast in the oven and eat them all up!

THE DRY STUFF
- 210 g flour, sifted
- 15 ml baking powder
- pinch of salt
- 60 ml castor sugar
- ½ teaspoon ground cardamom
- ½ teaspoon ground cinnamon

THE WET STUFF
- 1 jumbo egg
- 200 ml milk
- 15 ml sunflower oil

THE PUMPKIN
- 1 cup cooked butternut, mashed
- 1 small apple, peeled and finely chopped
- oil for shallow frying

Sift the dry stuff into a bowl, and beat the wet stuff together in a separate bowl. Make a well in the flour and stir in the wet stuff, mixing till nice and smooth.

Mix the mashed butternut and apple together well, and fold into the batter. If it seems a bit dry, just add a little more milk or even some water. If it seems too wet, add a little more flour. Let this rest for 30 minutes.

Heat the oil in a pot, or if you have a deep fryer use that. Check if the oil is ready by test-frying a cube of bread; it should brown quickly. When the oil is hot enough, cook spoonfuls of the batter till golden. Do this in batches and don't overcrowd the pot.

Serve with a sprinkle of cinnamon or vanilla sugar and a drizzle of honey. Enjoy!

SERVES 4 – 6

TIP: If you would like to ring the changes and have these as a savoury side dish, leave out the sugar from the dry stuff and add the following to the pumpkin mix: 1 teaspoon ground cumin, a chopped chilli, 2 cloves of crushed garlic, 4 finely chopped spring onions (with tops) and 1 teaspoon grated ginger. Once cooked, dust them with smoked paprika and salt – just a thought!

Easter chocolate chip crumpets

These chocolaty Easter crumpets are a tribute to the ones my Grandpa Bob made every day.

- 25 g butter
- 500 ml buttermilk
- 1 tablespoon honey
- 2 eggs
- 60 ml castor sugar
- 20 ml baking powder
- 500 ml sifted cake flour
- 100 g chocolate chips or 100 g 70 % dark chocolate

Melt the butter with half of the buttermilk and the honey over a low heat; then set aside to cool. Beat together the eggs and castor sugar. Mix the baking powder with the sifted flour in a large bowl, making a well in the centre of the flour.

Now add the remaining buttermilk to the egg mixture, and give it a good stir. Pour the buttermilk mixture into the flour and mix till smooth. Stir in the chocolate chips.

Lightly butter a non-stick frying pan and heat it. Now cook a few teaspoonfuls of crumpet mixture at a time. When the surface of the crumpets are covered with little air bubbles, turn them over and cook till golden on the other side.

SERVING SUGGESTIONS: Bananas just love chocolate, so spread the crumpets with Nutella and top with sliced bananas – the banana has to be fragrant and have freckles on its skin. Or try them topped with sliced banana, a few slices of crispy bacon, a blob of natural yoghurt and a drizzle of runny honey. Or just drop the bacon and keep the rest and serve as a dessert (or eat them for breakfast, what the heck!) with chocolate mascarpone cream.

SERVES 4 – 6

Coffee chocolate mascarpone cream

Great for topping crumpets or in pancakes served with toasted nuts and caramelised pears.

- 2 tablespoons coffee liqueur
- 250 g mascarpone cheese
- 200 g 70 % dark chocolate, melted

Stir the coffee liqueur into the mascarpone cheese, and then gently fold in the cooled melted chocolate. (Nobody needs to tell you that you can also eat this with a spoon!)

SERVES 4 – 6

Steamed haddock parcels

CHEESE SAUCE

- 1 litre milk
- 3 cloves garlic
- 2 tablespoons chopped onion
- 50 ml butter
- 50 ml flour
- 100 ml mature cheddar cheese, grated
- 3 tablespoons chopped fresh flat leaf parsley

FOR THE HADDOCK

- 4 large squares buttered greaseproof paper
- 4 cups raw baby spinach
- 4 portions haddock
- 16 cherry tomatoes, pan-fried till they pop

Make the sauce first. Warm the milk with the garlic and onion, and let it infuse while you make your roux. Strain the milk.

Make a roux by gently melting the butter in a pot and stirring in the flour. Gradually add the warm milk, stirring continuously to avoid lumps. Keep stirring until the sauce has thickened and is cooked. Add the cheese and stir until it has melted, then add the freshly chopped parsley. Set aside till needed. (Refrigerate if keeping overnight.)

To prepare the haddock, place the paper onto a flat surface and top with spinach. Place the haddock fillet onto that and seal up the parcel. Place into a steaming basket or in a colander over a pot of boiling water, and steam for 10 minutes.

Open the parcels and slide onto nice white plates, spoon over the cheese sauce and top with the cherry tomatoes. Serve with brown toast on the side and a couple of soft poached eggs.

SERVES 4

TIP: The parcels can be made the night before and kept in the fridge. To speed things up you can add boiled water to the pot and steam the haddock while you take a shower!

Panini filled with rocket, Brie, walnuts and bacon

- 1 panini per person, sliced open
- lots of fresh, peppery wild rocket
- lots of crispy, streaky bacon
- ripe Brie cheese
- toasted walnuts

Butter the bread if you like, but it's not really necessary as the cheese and bacon are quite rich. Now just fill it up to your heart's content and tuck in. These panini also make a great moveable feast, so just wrap up, pack into your picnic basket and off you go.

TIP: Keep in the fridge if you are making this up front, otherwise it will spoil.

Lots of bacon, crisply fried, and really ripe Brie is what's needed for this sarmie. There are no quantities for this recipe – just make a huge mother of a sandwich and wash it down with an ice-cold beer (it works well with the Brie and bacon).

CHAPTER TWO

Sensual *Salads*

From a very young age my sister Beverley and I used to spend our pocket money on a Saturday on bunches of turnips and carrots.

We would peel and slice and salt them, squeeze over lots of lemon juice, a sprinkle of curry powder and let them marinate. We would then, piece by glorious piece, divide up the salad into bowls, grab our books, get comfortable on our beds and nibble and suck away at the vegetables. I think this is when my love of developing salads began.

The last thing to wash over our taste buds was the yummy, turnipy, salty lemon juice, which we savoured. When we had extra money we added cashew nuts and sliced biltong – strange, some might say, when other children were spending their pocket money on sweets!

Mushroom, artichoke and roasted red pepper salad

Make this salad a day ahead, so that the flavours have time to mature. Most of us don't eat nearly enough raw mushrooms – they're delicious, packed with goodness and really low in fat. Artichokes are a member of the thistle family. They are said to be rich in antioxidants, high in fibre, great for your digestion, and contain a reasonable amount of folic acid.

THE DRESSING

- 1 teaspoon salt
- 2 tablespoons toasted coriander seeds
- ¾ cup red wine vinegar
- 1 cup olive oil
- 4 cloves garlic, peeled and crushed

THE SALAD

- 1 kg freshest, whitest, tightest button mushrooms you can find
- 1½ cups roughly chopped Italian parsley
- 2 x 410 g cans artichoke hearts, drained and cut in half
- 2 large red peppers, roasted and cut into strips
- 1 cluster enoki mushrooms, for decoration

First make the dressing. Place the salt, coriander seeds and wine vinegar in a saucepan. Bring to the boil and cook, uncovered, over high heat until it reduces to about 1 tablespoon of liquid. Remove from the stove. Add the olive oil and garlic, and give it a stir.

Next, wipe the mushrooms and halve them (don't ever wash them).

Pull half the parsley through the mushrooms and the other half through the artichokes. (I'm watching you: are you using your hands?)

Arrange the mushrooms in the bottom of your dish. Now pour the dressing over the artichokes and gently mix it in, using your hands. Put the artichokes on top of the mushrooms and cover.

After 6 hours, gently mix the mushrooms and artichokes together with the red peppers, using your hands so that you don't break up the ingredients.

When you are ready to serve, pile the salad onto a platter and drizzle with more olive oil and a good scattering of fresh parsley. Tuck a few beautiful enoki mushrooms into the salad to finish it off.

This salad is also great as a starter, served on a bed of rocket with grilled ciabatta on the side.

SERVES 8

DID YOU KNOW? The Greeks and Romans considered artichokes to be an aphrodisiac. The artichoke is technically a flower bud that has not yet bloomed.

"A woman is
like an artichoke;
you must work hard
to get to her heart."
Inspector Jacques Clouseau in 'The Pink Panther' (2006)

What a fine pear!

I love the combination of salty, sour goat's cheese with the sweetness of a pear in its prime, crisp and juicy and fragrant. I like to add nuts and seeds and peppery rocket, and I have a meal that makes my mouth love me!

FOR THE PEARS

- 6 firm ripe medium-sized pears, peeled and quartered
- 2 tablespoons extra virgin olive oil
- sea salt
- freshly ground black pepper
- ½ teaspoon ground cinnamon
- ½ teaspoon ground allspice
- 1 teaspoon finely chopped fresh ginger
- zest of 1 orange
- 1 tablespoon balsamic vinegar
- ½ teaspoon dried chilli flakes
- 1 teaspoon brown sugar

FOR THE SALAD

- 3 tablespoons extra virgin olive oil
- juice of 1 ripe lemon
- 150 g fresh rocket
- 300 g Fairview Chevin (goat's cheese)
- 2 spring onions with tops, thinly sliced
- ½ cup roughly chopped Italian parsley
- 80 g toasted pumpkin seeds
- 80 g toasted pecan nuts or hazelnuts

Place the pears in a glass bowl. Shake together the olive oil, salt and pepper, cinnamon, allspice, ginger, orange zest, balsamic vinegar, chilli flakes and brown sugar. Pour over the pears and marinate for 15 minutes.

Heat a large non-stick pan. Remove the pears from the marinade, reserving any left-over marinade for the dressing. Now caramelise the pears in the hot pan in small batches. Do not over-cook; we need the texture to keep our mouths happy!

Once all the pears are done, place the marinade, olive oil and lemon juice in the pan, bring to a gentle simmer and remove from the heat.

Put it together now – mix the pears and rocket together, and pile onto a platter. Top with goat's cheese, spring onion, parsley, pumpkin seeds and nuts, and drizzle the dressing over the salad. Yum!

SERVES 6

What could be more delicious than a meal made from really fresh, seasonal local ingredients? My mouth is ready to receive every time I walk past my newly-watered rocket bed and I think nothing of shoving a handful of freshly picked leaves into my mouth. Imported fruit and vegetables might add variety and interest to meals, but they come at a higher cost than seasonal ingredients, and they also have many more food miles under the belt!

Did you know?

Beetroot is a nutritious vegetable with so many health-giving properties. It is said to have a higher antioxidant content than most other vegetables.

It is also rich in vitamin C, fibre, potassium and magnesium, and the leafy tops are an excellent source of beta-carotene, iron and calcium ... so eat them!

Roasted beetroot salad

Delicious, earthy, ruby wedges of beetroot roasted and served with its tender stems and leaves, finished off with skordalia and toasted sesame seeds. I tasted this at the Greek Sizzler *in Johannesburg; this is my twist on it. Skordalia is a delicious Greek-style aïoli traditionally made with potatoes and garlic; but I have tasted it made with stale bread as well. I love this spooned over grilled aubergines, meat, fish, my face and everything!*

ROASTED BEETROOT
- 12 medium to large beetroots, with perfect leaves and stalks
- olive oil
- salt
- freshly ground black pepper

SKORDALIA
- 750 g potatoes
- 8 cloves garlic, mashed into a paste
- fresh lemon juice, to taste
- 175 – 200 ml extra virgin olive oil
- sea salt
- freshly ground black pepper
- 1 tablespoon toasted sesame seeds, for garnishing

Remove the stems and leaves from the beetroot. Thinly peel the beetroot and cut each into 8 wedges. Place the wedges onto an oven tray, drizzle with olive oil and season with salt and freshly ground black pepper. Roast them at 180 °C until they are just fork tender.

Now remove the leaves from the stalks and give them both a good wash – cook the stems in salted, boiling water till they are just tender, remove them and then blanch the leaves in the same water just till they wilt. Remove and drain.

Arrange the roasted beetroot wedges on a serving platter with the stems and leaves, and serve with the skordalia.

To make the skordalia, boil the potatoes in their skins until they are tender. While they are still warm and comfortable to handle, peel them and mash them.

Place the potatoes in a food processor with the remaining ingredients, except the sesame seeds, and blitz till smooth; season with salt and pepper. Taste and adjust the lemon juice and olive oil. Garnish with toasted sesame seeds.

SERVES 4 – 6

My garden is never without broad beans. I grow hundreds of the plants to keep me in a steady supply. So much of the broad bean plant is edible at different stages of its development. I often pick the beans when they are only half developed and the seeds in the pods are still small; I slice them with the pod, cook them lightly and toss them in garlic butter. I make delicious bean dips with them, and add them to stews. I pinch out about 10 cm of the growing tips and cook them like spinach – yummy! My friend Enzo Cocca taught me to lightly batter them and fry them – delicious!

I have the time of my life picking huge piles of beautiful fat swollen broad beans from my garden, munching as I go and thinking of all the wonderful things I can do with them. Please try this salad!

Broad bean, new potato and bacon salad with deep-fried leeks

THE SALAD
- 300 g new potatoes, boiled till tender, cooled and sliced
- 4 baby leeks, thinly sliced and deep-fried
- 250 g streaky bacon, crisply fried and chopped (keep the pan)
- 2 cups lightly steamed broad beans
- freshly ground black pepper
- salt, to taste

GARLIC THYME DRESSING
- ¾ cup extra virgin olive oil
- 3 cloves garlic, crushed
- 1 tablespoon fresh thyme leaves
- ¼ cup red wine vinegar
- 1 teaspoon wholegrain mustard
- 2 tablespoons freshly chopped chives

Place the potatoes, leeks, bacon and beans in a shallow dish, and season with black pepper and a little salt.

When mixing the dressing, pour the olive oil in the pan in which you cooked the bacon, add the garlic, thyme and vinegar to the pan and warm gently to lift off all the lovely bacon flavour. Remove from the heat and stir in the mustard and chives.

Pour the warm dressing onto the potatoes and beans, and stir gently to coat.

SERVES 4

TIP: When making a salad dressing, choose a good-quality vinegar; you don't want your guests gagging and choking from the fumes of a cheap and nasty version!

You can use red kidney beans or butter beans for the salad when broad beans are out of season.

Bean salad

THE SALAD
- 2 cans cannellini beans
- 2 cloves garlic, crushed
- 10 ml fresh lemon zest
- ½ cup roughly chopped Italian parsley with stems
- 2 teaspoons chopped preserved lemon
- 1 small red chilli, chopped (optional)

THE DRESSING
- 1 teaspoon cumin seeds, toasted and bashed
- ¾ teaspoon smoked paprika
- juice of 1 fresh ripe lemon
- 1 tablespoon grated onion
- salt and black pepper
- 3 tablespoons extra virgin olive oil

Please embrace the musical fruit! I know that most of us avoid eating beans for fear of an 'upside-down burp' accidently escaping, but the risk is so worth it. Healthy beans lower cholesterol, and are full of protein and dietary fibre.

Place the drained beans, garlic, zest, parsley, preserved lemon and chilli in a bowl. Mix all the dressing ingredients together, give them a good whisk, and dress the beans.

Mix together gently to coat the beans, and let this lie for about 2 hours before eating it so that the ingredients can get to know each other.

SERVES 4

Apple, red cabbage and courgette slaw

THE DRESSING
- 2 tablespoons red wine vinegar
- 1 tablespoon brown sugar
- 1 clove garlic, crushed
- 1 tablespoon honey
- 1 cup mayonnaise

THE SALAD
- 2 cups grated courgettes
- 2 green apples, cut into small squares
- 1 red onion, thinly sliced
- 1 ½ cups shredded red cabbage
- ½ cup raisins
- ¾ cup toasted sunflower seeds
- 1 tablespoon toasted caraway seeds

I could eat this every day for breakfast instead of muesli; the toasted caraway seeds impart a gentle liquorice flavour that pulls all the other flavours together!

Make the dressing by mixing the vinegar, brown sugar, garlic and honey together in a bowl. Stir in the mayonnaise, blending well.

Place all the salad ingredients in a large mixing bowl, stir the dressing gently through the salad, and transfer to a pretty serving platter.

SERVES 4

"Do not shame your salad by serving it undressed."

Anonymous

Mediterranean potato salad

- 6 potatoes, boiled in their jackets till just tender
- 3 ripe, firm tomatoes
- 1 red pepper, finely diced
- 1 small red onion, finely diced
- 4 spring onions with tops, thinly sliced
- 2 cloves garlic, peeled
- 1 cup flat leaf parsley, roughly chopped
- ½ cup freshly chopped mint
- 1 teaspoon Willow Creek basil infused olive oil
- 1 teaspoon Willow Creek lemon infused olive oil
- ½ cup Willow Creek extra virgin olive oil
- juice and zest of 1 fresh, ripe lemon
- salt
- freshly ground black pepper
- 3 rounds of feta cheese

Make this a few hours before you are going to serve it so all the flavours get to mingle. Also, don't over-cook the potatoes, they should be just cooked. This salad is something different and gets 10 out of 10 at every meal! And it is equally delicious for a few days after it is made.

Peel the potatoes and cut them into bite-sized cubes. Cut the tomatoes into quarters, remove the seeds and cut into small chunks. Put the tomato chunks in a bowl and mix in all the remaining ingredients, except the feta cheese, and let them marinate for an hour or so; this way they can get to know each other and the flavours can mingle.

Now layer the potatoes with the tomato mix in a glass bowl, cover and let the salad marinate for a further 2 hours. Just before you take it to the table, crumble the feta cheese roughly over the top of the salad and stir through lightly.

SERVES 6

TIP: I like to garnish the salad with a few tablespoons of deep-fried capers.

Ruby grapefruit and sprout salad

THE SALAD
- 4 ruby grapefruit, peeled without pith
- 4 spring onions with green tops, thinly sliced
- 1 cup mung bean sprouts
- ½ cup chickpea sprouts
- 1 cup thinly sliced deseeded cucumber

THE DRESSING
- ¼ cup soy sauce
- 2 teaspoons honey
- 1 teaspoon grated ginger
- 1 clove crushed garlic
- ¼ cup sunflower oil
- 1 teaspoon sesame oil
- 1 teaspoon toasted sesame seeds

Making a salad with ruby grapefruit is a clever way to include it in your diet. It tastes good, it is refreshing and it is packed with nutrients that cannot be found in other fruits. Lycopene from the bright red flesh and vitamin A are powerful antioxidants that help to boost the immune system – both are found in abundance in ruby grapefruit.

Separate the grapefruit into segments and place them in a glass bowl. Add the spring onions, sprouts and cucumber to the bowl.

Shake all the dressing ingredients together and pour over the grapefruit salad. Serve immediately or add some optional extras: ribbons of smoked salmon or trout; crispy fried bacon bits; little chunks of rare seared tuna; steamed prawn meat. Delicious!

SERVES 4

My blue heaven

- ½ cup good-quality mayonnaise
- ½ cup fresh cream
- ½ cup buttermilk or natural yoghurt
- 1 teaspoon Dijon mustard
- 1 clove garlic, crushed
- 1 tablespoon chopped flat leaf parsley
- 1 tablespoon chopped chives
- 1 tablespoon white balsamic vinegar
- salt and pepper
- ¾ cup toasted walnuts, roughly chopped
- 150 g Gorgonzola, Roquefort or Stilton
- a slice ciabatta per person
- 1 iceberg lettuce cut into 6 or 8 wedges
- extra walnuts for garnishing

Beautiful iceberg hearts, crisp and fresh, perched on a ciabatta crouton, and a dressing happy to hug all the naked greens. This salad is also great served with green beans as a side dish.

Place the mayonnaise, cream, buttermilk, mustard and garlic in a glass dish and mix together well. Just before serving the salad, stir in the parsley, chives, vinegar, salt and pepper, and the toasted walnuts. Crumble the blue cheese and stir it into the dressing.

Deep-fry the ciabatta slices till golden, and drain on paper towels. Arrange the iceberg wedges onto the ciabatta on a serving plate, spoon over the dressing, and sprinkle with the extra walnuts. Tuck in!

SERVES 6 – 8

TIP: Make a change and serve this salad as a fabulous BLT by adding chopped bacon and freshly sliced ripe tomato.

Pears, pecans and prunes with a gingered port dressing

I always peel the pears for this salad because the skins are quite tough. The addition of the blue cheese works well with the port dressing and enhances the flavour of the pecans, salty bacon and prunes.

THE DRESSING

- a little olive oil
- 5 cm fresh ginger, peeled and sliced into thin strips
- 3 cloves garlic, roughly chopped
- ½ cup runny honey
- 1 cup port
- ¼ cup rice wine vinegar
- a few drops of sesame oil
- salt
- freshly ground black pepper

FOR THE SALAD

- 18 pitted prunes, pre-soak in hot apple juice to cover
- 4 ripe but firm pears
- juice of 1 lemon
- 200 g toasted pecan nuts
- 1 small red onion, thinly sliced
- 2 large handfuls of fresh rocket
- 200 g blue-veined cheese, broken into small chunks
- 250 g streaky bacon, crisply fried (optional)

Make the dressing first. Heat about a tablespoon of olive oil in a small saucepan and fry the ginger for 1 minute. Add the garlic and cook till soft, but do not burn it. Add the honey and cook for a minute, stirring all the time.

Add the port and reduce down by half. Now, add the rice wine vinegar and the sesame oil – it is amazing how only a few drops add a special flavour to this dressing. Season with salt and black pepper. Taste and adjust the dressing with more vinegar if necessary.

Soak the prunes up front so that they are plump, soft and gooey when you are ready to make the salad.

Peel the pears and quarter them. Cut into thin slices, and sprinkle with some lemon juice to stop them from going brown.

Place the pears in a shallow bowl and add the nuts, prunes, onion, rocket and blue cheese (or Stilton – Mmmmm!) Toss the salad with the dressing and pile onto a white platter. Top with bacon and enjoy.

SERVES 6

TIP: Bear in mind that this is quite a sweet dressing and it works particularly well with the peppery flavour of the rocket, and salty bacon and blue cheese. If you love garlic as much as I do, you can crush a fresh clove into the dressing once it is cooked.

Broccoli, bacon and feta salad dressed in green

THE SALAD

- 1 kg fresh broccoli, stems peeled and broken into florets
- 1 cup crisply fried streaky bacon
- 4 slices of bread, cubed
- 1 small red onion, very thinly sliced

THE SAUCE

- 1 tablespoon capers
- 3 anchovy fillets
- 1 clove peeled garlic
- 1 cup Italian flat leaf parsley
- ½ cup fresh coriander
- ½ cup fresh basil
- 2 tablespoons pine nuts
- 1 teaspoon fresh lemon zest
- 1 tablespoon freshly grated Parmesan cheese
- ⅓ cup fresh lemon juice
- ⅔ cup extra virgin olive oil
- freshly ground black pepper

This is a new way to sneak broccoli into your family's diet. This amazing vegetable does not deserve to be plonked onto a plate in a soggy khaki lump; it is full of vitamins and minerals, and is an amazing non-dairy source of calcium.

Lightly steam the broccoli, and refresh in iced water. Slice the florets in half through the centre, and place in a bowl with the bacon.

Make the croutons by frying the bread cubes till golden, then drain on paper towels. Add to the bowl and top with sliced red onion.

Fling the sauce ingredients into a processor and give it a really good whizz. Taste for salt once the sauce is made, and then stir in some more if needed. Dress the salad with the sauce and toss well to coat. Serve immediately.

SERVES 4 – 6

TIP: To get the most health benefits from eating broccoli, it is important not to over-cook it. You need to preserve its nutrients and cancer-fighting compounds by steaming it lightly or by adding it to stir fries near the end of cooking.

A big green salad

- rocket
- all kinds of lettuce
- baby spinach
- fine green beans
- mange tout
- asparagus
- cucumber
- celery
- fresh mint
- parsley
- spring onions
- red onion
- dressing

Gather the greens you would like to put into your salad and 'lett–us' get started. I recommend the following …

Layer the leaves on a large, attractive serving platter. Scatter over the rest of the veggies and herbs, and top with some thin slivers of red onion to finish it off. Drizzle with your favourite dressing.

Make sure that all your ingredients are nice and dry so that your dressing clings to them!

SERVES 4

TIP: When making a salad, mix the textures and colours as this makes for a far more interesting salad. Always try to incorporate some green leafy vegetables, other than lettuce, in your salads as they are so rich in vitamin E and folate.

"It's difficult to think anything but pleasant thoughts while eating a home-grown tomato."
Lewis Grizzard

Dukkah, tomato and aubergine salad

Tahini paste is made from ground, roasted sesame seeds. If you can't find it at the supermarket, it is easy enough to make yourself – just pound together some sesame seeds and mix to a thick, smooth paste with a little olive oil.

THE DUKKAH
- 100 g blanched almonds
- 100 g white sesame seeds
- 20 g coriander seeds
- 50 g cumin seeds
- 1 teaspoon sea salt

THE SALAD
- 2 tablespoons tahini paste
- 1 clove crushed garlic
- ½ cup olive oil
- ½ cup fresh lemon juice
- salt and pepper, to taste
- 2 large aubergines, sliced into rounds and salted
- olive oil for frying
- 3 firm ripe tomatoes, sliced
- ½ preserved lemon, chopped
- ½ cup roughly chopped fresh coriander

To make the dukkah, toast the nuts and seeds in a hot, dry pan until fragrant, stirring all the time. Remove from the pan and cool. Grind coarsely with the sea salt and set aside.

Make a sauce to drizzle over the salad by mixing the tahini paste, garlic, olive oil and lemon juice; season with salt and pepper, and give it a good shake. If it is too thick, add a little warm water. Taste for seasoning and adjust if you need to; set aside till later.

Place the salted aubergine in a colander and let it sweat for 20 minutes. Rinse off the salt and pat dry. Heat some olive oil in a non-stick pan and fry the aubergine slices in batches; drain on paper towels.

Arrange a mixed layer of aubergine and tomato on a platter, sprinkle with some dukkah, preserved lemon and coriander, and drizzle with the tahini sauce. Serve immediately.

SERVES 4 – 6

My mom never had to tell us children that spinach was good for us. We always had it growing in the garden and she would stir it finely sliced through scrambled eggs and use the tiny little leaves in a salad. Spinach has lots of fibre, it's a fairly good source of iron and beta-carotene, and it has lots of potassium too. Raw spinach is a good source of vitamin C. So eat those greens!

Chorizo, spinach and deep-fried almond salad

THE SALAD
- 2 tablespoons olive oil
- 300 g chorizo sausage
- ½ teaspoon ground cinnamon
- 2 cloves crushed garlic
- 100 g whole blanched almonds
- 2 large potatoes, peeled, boiled and cubed
- 300 g washed baby spinach
- 1 red onion, thinly sliced
- Parmesan cheese shavings

THE DRESSING
- 1 teaspoon cumin seeds, toasted and bashed
- 1 clove crushed garlic
- ⅓ cup fresh lemon juice
- ⅔ cup olive oil
- salt and black pepper
- ½ teaspoon chopped mint
- 1 tablespoon chopped Italian parsley

Heat the olive oil in a frying pan. Cut the sausage into rings and fry with the cinnamon and garlic till it takes on some colour. Remove with a slotted spoon and set aside in a dish.

Add the almonds to the same pan and cook for 1 minute; remove and add to the sausage. If there is not enough oil left in the pan, add a little more and fry the potatoes. Add them to the dish.

Arrange the spinach leaves on a serving platter. Scatter the sausage, almonds and potatoes over the leaves, and top with the onion slices.

Make the dressing by placing all the ingredients in a jar with a tight-fitting lid. Give it all a hearty shake and, before pouring it over the salad, taste and adjust the seasoning.

Garnish generously with Parmesan shavings and serve.

SERVES 6

TIP: I sometimes leave out the potatoes and instead add two cups of butter beans to this salad to ring the changes. It works well with couscous too.

Roasted tomato and butter bean salad with whole roasted garlic

FOR THE TOMATOES

- 500 g Rosa or cherry tomatoes
- 12 whole cloves garlic, peeled
- 1 teaspoon brown sugar
- 2 tablespoons fresh rosemary needles
- salt
- freshly ground black pepper
- olive oil

THE DRESSING

- ⅔ cup extra virgin olive oil
- ⅓ cup fresh lemon juice
- salt and pepper to taste

FOR THE SALAD

- 250 g streaky bacon, crisply fried and finely chopped
- zest of 1 fresh lemon
- 8 spring onions with tops, finely sliced
- 1 cup fresh Italian parsley, roughly chopped
- 2 tablespoons capers
- ½ cup pitted black olives, roughly chopped
- ½ cup fresh sweet basil, torn
- 2 cans butter beans, drained and lightly rinsed

Sticky rosemary tomatoes, salty crispy bacon and creamy butter beans that won't put too much wind into your sails.

Place the tomatoes, garlic, brown sugar and rosemary in a glass bowl. Season with salt and pepper and add a good glug of olive oil. Toss well to coat. Pour the lot onto an oven tray and roast at 190 °C till wrinkly and taking on a little colour.

While the tomatoes are roasting make the dressing. Put all the dressing ingredients into a glass jar and shake the hell out of it.

Then place the salad ingredients in a large bowl and coat with the dressing. When the tomatoes are roasted, scrape them out of the pan and toss them, using your hands, into the beans. Don't leave any of the oil behind and yes, you do get to eat the garlic! (You are allowed to let them cool a bit; don't want you burning yourself now.)

Let the salad rest for at least an hour and a half before you serve it, allowing the flavours to mature.

SERVES 4 – 6

This wild rice salad is for my dear, darling friend Myrna Wittels, who is the size of a matchstick and could eat this whole bowl herself ... well almost! When I talk about chopped spring onions in my recipes, the entire onion, except the root, is used.

Wild rice and barley salad

THE SALAD
- 1 cup brown rice
- ½ cup wild rice
- ¾ cup barley
- oil for deep frying
- 3 leeks, thinly sliced
- 2 red sweet peppers, roasted
- ½ cup chopped sultanas
- ½ cup chopped dried Turkish apricots
- ½ cup roughly chopped dried cranberries
- ½ cup roughly chopped Italian parsley
- extra parsley for garnishing
- 1 cup toasted cashew nuts
- ½ cup toasted pine nuts
- 6 spring onions with tops, chopped

THE DRESSING
- 3 cloves garlic, crushed
- ¾ cup olive oil
- juice and zest of 1 lemon
- juice and zest of 1 orange
- salt and freshly ground pepper, to taste

Cook the brown rice separately until al dente; drain and cool. Then boil the wild rice in a little water till just cooked; strain and cool. Soak the barley in some water to cover, and steam lightly till just tender. Mix both the brown and wild rice together with the barley in a large bowl.

Deep-fry the leeks in batches and stir into the cooked grain. Cut the peppers into strips and add them to the bowl. Stir in the remaining ingredients.

Mix the dressing ingredients together well, and stir into the rice salad. Cover and leave in the fridge for 24 hours.

Adjust the seasoning, if necessary, just before you serve it; you might want to add more lemon juice.

SERVES 6 – 8

Chicken and pancetta salad

- 4 chicken breasts
- 2 cos lettuces, washed
- 250 g pancetta, crisply fried
- 6 spring onions with tops, chopped
- 1 tablespoon roughly chopped mint
- 3 sticks table celery, thinly sliced
- 1 large handful wild rocket
- ½ cup pine nuts, toasted
- 1 ripe pineapple, peeled and cut into chunks
- 150 g fresh mozzarella, torn into pieces
- 1 can artichoke hearts, sliced

This is not a salad. It is a main course served with chunks of crusty bread and lots of olive oil, a glass of what you like really chilled, and some good company.

Slow roast the chicken on the bone (with the skin on). Cool and slice. Tear the cos lettuces into 3 (don't use a knife) and place on a serving platter. Arrange all the salad ingredients onto the bed of cos lettuce and serve. This salad doesn't really need any dressing as it is so nice with just the olive oil, but you can splash it with a little balsamic vinegar and olive oil if you like.

SERVES 4 – 6

TIP: Bacon can be substituted for the pancetta, or you can leave the bacon out if you don't do piggy.

Nutty radish salad

THE DRESSING
- 1 teaspoon English mustard powder
- 2 cloves crushed garlic
- salt and black pepper
- 2 teaspoons toasted cumin seeds, roughly ground
- juice of ⅓ lemon
- ⅔ cup extra virgin olive oil

THE SALAD
- 2 large handfuls fresh mint
- 2 large handfuls coriander
- 2 large handfuls fresh flat leaf parsley
- ½ cup chopped almonds
- ½ cup chopped pecan nuts
- 3 cups young-crop radishes, sliced and chilled
- zest of 1 ripe lemon
- 2 tablespoons toasted sesame seeds

This is a freshly chopped salad, so fragrant and healthy. Please try it!

For the dressing, blitz all the ingredients together in a blender up front, allowing the flavours to merge while you prepare the salad.

For the salad, make sure that your herbs are as fresh as ever and very well washed. The stems of the herbs are used as well, so don't dare throw them out, okay! Now that we're on the same page, let's get started.

Make sure the herbs are dry before you chop them roughly. Toast the nuts lightly. Toss the herbs together with half the nuts, the radish slices, lemon zest and sesame seeds. Just before you bring the salad to the table, dress it and scatter over the remaining nuts.

SERVES 4

I grew up eating radishes from a very young age; we always had them in our garden. They grow fast and I just love eating these spicy little red balls, freshly picked while they are young and crisp, with a shake of salt!

Roast butternut and Parmesan crisp salad

Yummy – all rosemary-infused and sticky, sweet and salty!

- 8 tablespoons grated
  Parmesan cheese
- 1 long-necked butternut,
  well washed
- ½ cup rosemary needles
- olive oil, to drizzle
- brown sugar
- salt, to taste
- 3 tablespoons toasted
  pumpkin seeds
- a shake of cinnamon
- honey for drizzling

TIP: Don't discard the butternut seeds - wash them off and roast them, or plant them, or give them to your parrot if you have one (my African Greys just love any kind of pumpkin seeds). Pumpkin seeds are high in zinc, and rich in iron and omega 3 essential fatty acids, so eat them often!

Preheat the oven to 200 °C.

Place 8 heaps of grated Parmesan cheese on a lightly-greased oven tray and place under the grill until the cheese has melted and started to colour lightly. Remove the tray from the oven and leave the Parmesan to cool and crisp up.

Give the butternut a good wash and then slice it very thinly, with the skin still on, and pack the slices onto oven trays so that they do not overlap. Sprinkle with the rosemary needles. Drizzle very lightly with olive oil - it is important not to over-oil the butternut slices as they become soggy and don't get crisp. Give the slices a sprinkling of brown sugar and a little shower of salt.

Roast until they are crispy and curling. Remove from the oven and pack onto a platter with the Parmesan crisps. Scatter with toasted pumpkin seeds and finish off with a light dusting of cinnamon and a drizzle of honey.

SERVES 4

"Cheese – milk's leap toward immortality."
Clifton Fadiman

CHAPTER THREE

Soupa *Sensory*

I cherish the memories of the first time I taste a new food. My philosophy is that you should never cut yourself off from trying something just because it looks or smells strange and different. If you do, you will never know what you are missing out on, and you might just love it.

I've tried things where I've thought, 'Oh my god! I can't bear it!' My first taste of halloumi, for example. When I saw that murky white stuff floating in these big jars I thought there was no way I would eat it. My friend's Greek granny said, '*Fáō, fáō, fáō!*' which means 'Eat, eat, eat!' and I can still taste that gorgeous, caramelised, salty cheese. It was warm and every time I bit into it, it stretched and my body just wanted to dance it tasted so good.

You know how it happens ... you start humming ... Mmmm, Mmmm ... and then you start moving your head, then your hands, then your whole body starts to dance while you're eating.

I just love halloumi now – I sometimes even toss it on top of a bowl of thick, chunky soup.

"Soup is
liquid comfort."
Author unknown

Quick mushroom soup

- 2 tablespoons butter
- 2 leeks, white part only, thinly sliced
- 3 cloves garlic, finely chopped
- 1 carrot, peeled and finely diced
- 1 stick celery, finely sliced
- 1 kg button mushrooms
- 1 level teaspoon dried tarragon
- 2 tablespoons brown sherry
- 1 cup chicken stock
- 2 cups milk
- seaweed salt and black pepper
- ½ cup fresh cream
- 4 tablespoons snipped chives

Heat the butter in a saucepan and cook the leeks, garlic, carrot and celery till they are wilted. Add the mushrooms and tarragon and cook till the mushrooms soften, stirring all the while. Add the sherry and cook for 2 minutes. Add the chicken stock and simmer for 10 minutes, then add the milk and cook for 1 minute. Season with salt and pepper, and remove from the heat.

Transfer to a liquidiser and blitz till smooth, adding more milk if necessary. Return to the saucepan and heat through gently. Stir in the cream and chives, and serve.

SERVES 4 – 6

TIP: Never wash a mushroom; it is grown in sterile conditions and just needs to be brushed clean.

Smoked paprika potato soup

A touch of smoked paprika gives this soup a wonderful lift, and the salty bacon and fresh thyme just brings it all together. Wish I was there to see you happily slurping away!

- 2 tablespoons olive oil
- 5 leeks, white part only, finely sliced
- 5 cloves crushed garlic
- 4 large potatoes, peeled and thinly sliced
- 2 teaspoons fresh thyme leaves
- ¾ teaspoon smoked paprika
- 800 g chopped tinned tomatoes
- 1 litre chicken stock
- salt
- freshly ground black pepper
- ⅓ cup roughly chopped soup celery leaves
- extra 1 teaspoon fresh thyme leaves
- 1 cup chopped crispy streaky bacon

Heat the olive oil in a large saucepan. Add the leeks, garlic, potato, thyme and smoked paprika, and cook gently until soft, without browning please! Add the tomatoes and cook for 5 minutes. Then add the stock and cook for a further 15 minutes, giving it a good stir every so often.

Season with salt and pepper and cook for 10 minutes more. Add the chopped celery leaves and extra thyme.

Ladle the soup into bowls, top with crispy bacon and serve with crusty French bread. (Onion bread is also delicious with this soup.)

SERVES 6 – 8

TIP: Cubes of deep-fried halloumi cheese can be used instead of bacon, or why not use both? If you are using halloumi cheese, soak it for 10 minutes to remove some of the salt, and then drain and dry it very well before you fry it – the cheese is deliciously crisp on the outside and soft on the inside.

"In the childhood memories of every cook, there is a large kitchen, a warm stove, a simmering pot and a mom."
Barbara Costikyan

Chinese broth with beef fillet

THE BROTH

- 3 onions, peeled and sliced
- 4 carrots, peeled and sliced
- 4 celery stalks, sliced
- 2 cm fresh ginger, cut into thin strips
- 2 cloves garlic, crushed
- 1 leek, sliced
- 2 whole star anise pods
- 10 black peppercorns
- 2 dried cloves
- 2 litres good-quality ready-made chicken or vegetable stock
- salt
- freshly ground black pepper

BITS FOR THE BOWL

- 200 g fillet steak
- 1 large carrot, cut into very small cubes
- 3 cm fresh ginger, cut into very thin matchsticks
- 2 red chillies, deseeded and thinly sliced
- 2 spring onions with tops, finely sliced
- 1 cup mung bean sprouts
- 1 handful coriander, roughly chopped

TO FINISH OFF

- sesame oil
- soy sauce
- 1 cup cubed silken tofu (optional)

Heat a little oil in a large pot and fry the onions, carrots, celery, ginger, garlic and leek until soft and fragrant; about 4 minutes. Add the spices and the stock, and simmer gently for 40 minutes, skimming off any impurities as they rise to the surface. Strain and reheat when you need it.

Prepare all the extra bits and pieces while the broth is simmering. Season the fillet steak with salt and white pepper. Sear it, leaving it very rare, and rest till needed.

Just before you are ready to serve, slice the fillet very thinly and divide into 4 portions. Place a portion of fillet in the bottom of each soup bowl, and top with a little of each of the bits for the bowl.

Season the strained broth with salt and freshly ground black pepper, heat it up and pour the very hot stock into the soup bowls. Finish off with a sprinkling of sesame oil and soy sauce, and enjoy. Now why don't you add a little tofu? Go on, do it – I do!

SERVES 4

EXTRAS: I love to add pre-soaked sliced shiitake mushrooms and cloud ear mushrooms to the boiling stock after it is strained – please try it as well! I use half a cup dried cloud ear and 6 dried shiitake – they expand like crazy. So if you do want to add the mushrooms, soak them in warm water till they are soft and plump, then chop or slice them the way you want them to feel in your mouth, and add them to the strained hot stock.

"There is nothing like soup. It is by nature eccentric: no two are ever alike, unless of course you get your soup in a can."
Laurie Colwin

Chickpea and roasted tomato soup

This chunky, wholesome soup is a meal in a bowl.

THE TOMATO BIT

- 2 kg really ripe tomatoes, quartered
- 12 cloves garlic, peeled
- 3 red peppers, quartered and seeded
- olive oil
- ½ teaspoon sugar
- salt

THE CHUNKY BIT

- 2 cups raw chickpeas, soaked
- 3 tablespoons olive oil
- 1 teaspoon cumin seeds, toasted and bashed
- 2 onions, chopped
- ½ teaspoon chilli flakes
- 4 chicken thighs, without skin
- 1 litre chicken stock
- salt, to taste
- freshly ground black pepper
- 2 teaspoons fresh thyme leaves

Fling all the ingredients for the tomato bit together on an oven tray and roast for 45 minutes at 180 °C. You will smell when it is ready; if the tomatoes are all wrinkly and sweet smelling, remove from the oven and cool.

Blend the tomato mixture until it is really beaten up, and then push it through a sieve. Keep to one side until needed.

Now get stuck into the chunky bit. Soak the chickpeas in cold water till they soften – it is best to soak them overnight, or for a minimum of two hours if you didn't plan ahead. Rinse them, put them in a pot of cold water, bring to the boil and then simmer until they are tender; about 25 minutes.

Heat the olive oil, add the cumin and cook for 1 minute, stirring all the time. Add the onions and chilli flakes, and cook for 5 minutes, giving it a stir every so often. Do not brown the onions! Now you can add the chicken; cook for 7 minutes.

Add the cooked chickpeas and stir to coat. Add the stock and continue to cook till the chicken is tender and cooked through, do not over-cook!

Remove the chicken and stir in the strained tomatoes. Season with salt and pepper, add the thyme and heat through. Then chop up the chicken and stir it into the soup.

SERVES 6

TIP: I like to stir in a half a teaspoon of toasted, bashed cumin seeds as I heat up the soup. In fact, I highly recommend it!

Lamb and barley soup

THE SOUP

- 3 tablespoons olive oil
- salt
- freshly ground black pepper
- 300 g lamb knuckle
- 2 large onions, chopped
- 2 leeks, chopped
- 1 large carrot, chopped
- 1 cup chopped celery
- 1 tablespoon fresh thyme leaves
- 3 cloves garlic, chopped
- 1 fresh bay leaf
- 8 tablespoons pearl barley
- 2 potatoes, peeled and cubed
- 8 cups chicken stock

THE TOPPING

- ½ cup freshly chopped flat leaf parsley
- 1 teaspoon lemon zest
- 1 clove garlic, crushed
- 10 celery leaves, finely chopped
- ½ cup freshly grated Parmesan cheese

Heat the oil in a large frying pan and season the lamb knuckle. Fry till golden brown; remove from the pan and add the onions, leeks, carrot, celery, thyme, garlic and bay leaf. Fry gently for 5 minutes and add a few tablespoons of chicken stock to the pot to prevent it from catching.

Add the barley, potatoes and chicken stock, and adjust the seasoning. Return the lamb to the pot and simmer the soup gently for 2 hours. Add more liquid if needed!

Just before serving, stir all the topping ingredients together. Ladle the soup into bowls and top with spoonfuls of topping.

SERVES 4 – 6

Chunky butternut, sweet potato and chicken soup

I love to stir a few spoons of cardamom rice into my soup when I feel like real comfort food!

THE BASE

- 3 tablespoons sunflower oil
- 2 onions, finely chopped
- 1 stick lemon grass, soft centre only, finely chopped
- 3 cloves garlic, crushed
- 2 teaspoons grated ginger
- 1 teaspoon ground cumin
- ½ teaspoon ground coriander
- 1 teaspoon curry powder
- freshly ground black pepper
- ¾ teaspoon turmeric
- 1 teaspoon brown sugar
- 1 ½ litres chicken stock

THE BALANCE

- 1 cup cubed butternut
- 1 cup cubed sweet potato
- 1 can coconut milk
- 2 chicken breasts, thinly diced
- fresh coriander, chopped

Heat the oil in a large pot and add the onions, lemon grass, garlic, ginger, cumin, coriander, curry powder, pepper, turmeric and brown sugar. Cook slowly until the mixture becomes fragrant – about 8 to 10 minutes.

Add a little chicken stock to prevent the spices from burning, and cook for a further 5 minutes. Add the rest of the chicken stock and simmer till the onions are soft. Liquidise until smooth.

If the base is too thick, add another cup of liquid and bring the stock to a gentle boil before adding the balance of the ingredients. Add the butternut and sweet potato, and simmer for 10 minutes. Then add the coconut milk and chicken, and simmer till the vegetables are fork tender.

Stir in some chopped coriander and serve.

SERVES 4 – 6

Did you know?

Sweet potatoes are low in fat, high in vitamin E, antioxidants, iron, minerals, beta-carotene, potassium and lots more.

Broccoli and feta soup

I always use the broccoli stems. I add them before the florets, so they all cook perfectly.

- 1 kg fresh broccoli
- 1 litre good chicken stock
- 1 tablespoon butter
- 1 potato, peeled and diced
- 1 onion, peeled and diced
- 1 teaspoon crushed garlic
- 1 teaspoon fresh thyme leaves
- ½ cup fresh cream
- salt and black pepper
- feta cheese, crumbled

TIP: If your soup looks a little dull, add a handful of fresh spinach or frozen peas to the blender when liquidising it, and it will lift the colour!

Break the broccoli into florets and peel the stems (set a few stems aside to add near the end). Heat the stock and blanch the broccoli in the stock, adding the reserved stems. Remove the broccoli from the pot and take the stock from the stove.

In a frying pan, heat the butter and cook the potato, onion, garlic and thyme till the onions and potatoes are soft. Moisten with a little of the chicken stock if need be.

Liquidise the broccoli with the chicken stock and onion mix till smooth (without it blowing up in your face of course – keep your hand on the lid – been there done that).

Pour the soup into a saucepan and heat gently. Season with salt and pepper, stir in the cream and serve garnished with crumbled feta and a little swirl of extra virgin olive oil if you like.

SERVES 4 – 6

Corn and chicken soup

- 2 litres homemade chicken stock
- olive oil
- 1 level teaspoon five-spice powder
- 1 tablespoon finely chopped fresh ginger
- 3 cloves garlic, crushed
- 3 cups fresh sweet corn kernels
- 4 chicken breast fillets, thinly sliced
- 1 can creamed sweet corn
- 1 teaspoon cornflour mixed with ½ cup water
- 2 cups sliced spring onions
- 1 cup thinly sliced celery with leaves
- 1 cup bean sprouts
- sesame oil for drizzling
- soy sauce for splashing

You need to get a kick-ass pot of homemade chicken stock simmering gently on the stove.

Heat a little oil in a large pot and fry the five-spice powder, ginger and garlic for a few minutes to release the flavour; don't burn it now! Add the chicken stock and cook for 10 minutes with the lid off.

Add the fresh corn kernels and cook for 8 minutes, then add the chicken breasts and canned sweet corn, and cook for 7 minutes more on a low heat. Pour in enough cornflour mix to thicken the soup to your taste. Add the spring onions and celery, and cook for 5 minutes. Check the seasoning and add a little salt if necessary. Ladle into bowls, top with sprouts, and add sesame oil and soy sauce to taste.

TIP: Add a little chilli and coriander to the soup if you like; I must say, I like!

SERVES 6 – 8

Smooth creamy liquid, thick and chunky with chicken and corn; this is a real comfort meal and so satisfying.

Cream of celery, potato, lettuce and bacon soup

- 2 tablespoons butter
- 1 teaspoon olive oil
- 2 onions, peeled and finely chopped
- 2 teaspoons chicken stock powder (choose one with no MSG)
- 3 cloves fresh garlic, chopped
- 3 potatoes, peeled and cut into small cubes
- 5 sticks celery, sliced
- 2 cups hot water
- 1 tablespoon fresh thyme leaves
- 1 cup frozen peas
- ½ iceberg lettuce with outer leaves, shredded
- 1 cup fresh celery leaves
- 1 litre warm milk
- salt
- freshly ground black pepper
- a good shake of smoked paprika
- ½ cup fresh cream
- ½ cup grated Gruyere cheese
- 1 cup streaky bacon, chopped and cooked till crisp

My garden has soup celery growing everywhere. I could not live without it.

Heat the butter and olive oil in a large saucepan. Add the onions and chicken stock powder, and cook gently till the onions wilt. Stir the garlic, potatoes and celery into the onions and cook for 5 minutes, stirring all the while. Add half the hot water and simmer gently for 5 minutes, then add the remaining hot water, fresh thyme, peas and lettuce, and cook till the lettuce just wilts. Stir in the celery leaves and remove from the heat.

Liquidise in two batches with the warm milk, till smooth. Taste for seasoning and return to a clean saucepan, and heat gently with a shake of smoked paprika. If the soup is too thick for you, thin with a little more milk and adjust the seasoning.

Stir in the cream and the cheese; spoon into bowls and top with bacon bits. Serve with crusty bread or spicy croutons.

SERVES 4

TIP: If you want a smoother soup, you can pass it through a sieve before reheating it.

Spicy croutons

Never waste a slice of bread – make some spicy croutons for soups and salads! You can make as many as you think you will need, and there's no need to deep-fry.

Heat the oven to 180 °C. Brush olive oil over slices of French bread, ciabatta or ordinary sliced bread, then cut each slice into 4 or more. Shake over some smoked paprika, chilli powder and a little salt, and bake on a baking tray till golden and crisp.

Rich pea soup with pork dumplings

THE SOUP

- 1 cup split peas
- 2 tablespoons olive oil
- 2 leeks, chopped
- 1 large onion, diced
- 3 cloves crushed garlic
- 4 stalks celery, chopped
- 4 rashers streaky bacon, chopped
- 2 tablespoons butter
- 2 teaspoons fresh thyme leaves
- 8 cups chicken stock
- 2 ¾ cups frozen peas
- ½ cup chopped parsley

PORK DUMPLINGS

- 300 g pork mince
- 2 spring onions with tops, finely chopped
- 2 cloves garlic, chopped
- 1 teaspoon chopped fresh ginger
- 2 tablespoons chopped parsley
- ½ cup fresh breadcrumbs
- salt
- freshly ground pepper
- ½ teaspoon ground allspice

I love a dumpling of any kind. The secret to making a good dumpling is to mind your own business until it is time to lift the lid. Do not lift the lid too soon!

Soak the split peas in hot water for 30 minutes. Heat the oil in a very large saucepan and gently cook the leeks, onion, garlic, celery and bacon for 5 minutes. Now stir in the butter and thyme and cook, stirring for another 5 minutes.

Add the split peas and stock, and cook till the peas are very soft, adding more liquid if needed.

In the meantime, make the dumplings. Mix all the ingredients together and roll into walnut-sized balls. Chill till you need them.

Liquidise the soup in batches with 2 cups of the frozen peas, and return to the pot. Bring to a simmer and add the pork dumplings. Simmer covered till they are cooked; for 15 minutes or so. Stir in the remaining frozen peas and parsley, and serve.

SERVES 6

TIP: Fry some of the pork mince to check the seasoning before you roll it into dumplings. You can use chicken or beef instead of pork, if you prefer.

Chilled tomato soup scented with sweet basil

There is something about a bowl of chilled tomato soup that screams, 'Summer is here!' How about adding some crispy bacon bits, golden croutons, Parmesan shavings and snipped chives?

- 1 tablespoon olive oil
- 1 onion, peeled and chopped
- 2 cloves garlic, crushed
- 3 cups vegetable stock
- 1.5 kg really ripe tomatoes, skinned and chopped
- 1 teaspoon castor sugar
- salt
- freshly ground black pepper
- 250 ml buttermilk
- ½ English cucumber, peeled and chopped
- ½ cup fresh basil
- ½ – 1 green chilli, seeds removed and chopped
- ½ cup tomato pesto

Heat the olive oil in a saucepan and gently fry the onion and garlic; don't brown. When they are soft and translucent, add the vegetable stock, tomatoes and castor sugar, and simmer down gently. Season with salt and pepper

Liquidise the soup with the buttermilk, cucumber, fresh basil, chilli and tomato pesto. Adjust the seasoning and add a little more sugar if you wish. Chill till needed.

Ladle the soup into bowls and, if you like, pile on the bacon, croutons, masses of Parmesan and snipped chives. If you would like to make the soup a little richer, add a couple of splashes of fresh cream and a clove of crushed garlic.

SERVES 4

Quick chilled gazpacho with bits on the side

GAZPACHO

- 2 litres tomato juice
- 1 red pepper, chopped
- ½ English cucumber, chopped
- 3 sticks celery, chopped
- 1 thick slice crustless white bread, crumbed
- zest and juice of 1 very ripe lemon
- 1 tablespoon red wine vinegar
- 2 tablespoons chopped fresh coriander
- Tabasco sauce to taste
- 3 tablespoons olive oil
- salt
- freshly ground black pepper

Place the gazpacho ingredients in a food processor in batches, and whizz till smooth. Strain and season with salt and pepper, and chill till needed.

Place a selection of bits and pieces into individual bowls, and serve alongside the soup; each person can then add the bits they like best. How about these:

- ½ English cucumber, diced
- 1 red pepper, diced
- 1 green pepper, diced
- 2 cups of deep-fried croutons
- 150 g feta cheese, roughly crumbled
- small bowl basil pesto

SERVES 8

TIP: To skin tomatoes, make a small cross on the bottom of each tomato and plunge into boiling water. The skins will just slide off – I just love squishing off those skins.

CHAPTER FOUR

Using your *Noodle*?

When I was very young, in Grade One, we lived in a house called Holly Villa in Durban, and I had a friend called Paula who lived down the road. It was through her that I was first introduced to Parmesan cheese.

When I went to play at her house for the first time my immediate impression was, 'Oh no! This house smells of vomit!' Coming up the stairs, that smell was so strong. Her mother said we should sit down and have some lunch, and that was my first encounter with risotto.

I had such a problem bringing that spoon up to my mouth because I realised where the smell was coming from – the dish in front of me! We were brought up to always eat everything on our plates, especially when we were guests in someone else's home. So I looked at the gorgeous, creamy-looking rice and thought, 'Okay, here goes.'

I swallowed that first mouthful so fast I don't think it even touched sides, and I was holding my breath so I couldn't smell it. But somewhere along the line something must have touched a taste bud because as I got my breath back that flavour hit me and, oh my god, what a taste! After that I shovelled it in and asked for more.

And the rest, as they say, is history. I have been eating it ever since.

Mussel meat and leek risotto topped with prawns

In case you have never made risotto with me before, I like to do it like this. You need time and patience for making a risotto; it's like foreplay. You spend a lot of time at the pot, keeping it moist and when all the wet stuff cooks away, wet it again. The end result should be creamy and tender – well worth the time spent! So get your glass of wine … and stay with the heat.

- 2 teaspoons olive oil
- 3 tablespoons butter
- 1 onion, peeled and finely chopped
- 3 leeks, white part only, thinly sliced
- 2 cloves garlic, crushed
- 1 cup uncooked risotto rice
- 5 cups boiling chicken stock
- ½ cup dry white wine
- ⅓ cup grated Parmesan
- 300 g mussel meat
- 200 g prawn meat
- ¾ cup cream
- ½ cup roughly chopped Italian parsley
- 3 tablespoons snipped chives
- salt and pepper, to taste

Heat the olive oil and butter in a saucepan and fry the onion and leeks gently till they are soft – don't burn them! When translucent, add the garlic and rice, and stir well to coat the rice.

Add a third each of the stock and the wine, stirring constantly. Simmer until almost all the liquid has been absorbed. Repeat until the stock and wine have all been used and the rice is tender. Cooking time should be 35 to 40 minutes.

Stir in the Parmesan cheese, and mussel and prawn meat. Add the cream, and warm the mussels and prawns through. Stir in the herbs, season with salt and pepper, and serve. I like to enrich it with a spoon of butter and then serve with a huge green salad.

SERVES 4

TIP: Keep the stock hot at all times. I love to add little cubes of roasted red pepper to this risotto as a garnish.

Did you know?

Once rice has been cooked, you have to take good care of it. If rice left from your dinner has stood at room temperature overnight, bacteria will have a field day; they will multiply at an alarming rate and cause food-poisoning toxins that will leave you sick and weak from vomiting and diarrhoea, so throw out any rice that has been left out overnight!

If you want to reuse any leftovers the next day to make egg-fried rice, run some cold water through the rice, bag it and put it into the fridge straightaway. Remember that bacteria can make you really ill; do not keep cooked rice for longer than two days in the fridge and never reheat it more than once.

"Without rice, even the cleverest housewife cannot cook."
Chinese proverb

Pineapple and chicken rice with cashews

- 12 large spinach leaves (Swiss chard)
- 2 tablespoons vegetable oil
- 250 g diced chicken
- 1 teaspoon chopped ginger
- 2 cloves garlic, chopped
- 2 spring onions with tops, sliced
- 1 stem lemon grass, finely chopped
- 1 small chilli, chopped
- 1 teaspoon fish sauce
- 1 tablespoon soy sauce
- ½ cup chopped fresh pineapple
- ½ cup toasted chopped cashews
- ¾ cup cooked sticky rice
- ½ cup coconut milk
- sweet chilli sauce

Remove the stalks from the spinach. Blanch the leaves and do not break – refresh in iced water.

Heat the oil in a frying pan and fry the chicken, ginger, garlic and spring onions. Once the chicken changes colour, add the lemon grass and chilli, and stir through. Then add the fish sauce and soy sauce; cook, stirring for 1 minute. Stir in the pineapple, nuts, rice and coconut milk.

Lay the spinach leaves on a flat work surface. Place a portion of the chicken rice onto the spinach, roll up to cover the rice, fold in the sides and finish rolling. Serve with sweet chilli sauce.

SERVES 4, OR 6 AS A STARTER

TIP: When I use lemon grass in a recipe, I only chop the bottom third into the dish.

Spinach rice with artichokes and pine nuts

I usually make this as a light lunch dish and serve it with a salad made from as many fresh veggies as I can find in my fridge.

- ½ cup olive oil, for cooking
- 4 large leeks, washed, dried and roughly chopped
- 3 cloves garlic, crushed
- 500 g spinach, well washed, dried and roughly chopped
- 4 cups cooked long-grain rice
- salt and black pepper
- juice of 1 large lemon
- ½ cup Italian parsley, chopped
- 4 tablespoons pine nuts
- 1 x 400 g can artichokes, drained and roughly chopped
- 1 green chilli, chopped (optional)

Heat the olive oil in a large saucepan, add the leeks and garlic, and cook gently till the leeks are almost soft, not brown. Add the spinach and cook till it wilts then stir in the rice. Season with salt and pepper, and set aside.

Squeeze in the lemon juice and stir in the parsley, pine nuts, artichokes and chilli.

Pile into a deep white bowl, top with shavings of Parmesan cheese and serve with some lemon wedges.

SERVES 6

SERVING TIPS: If serving as a vegetarian dish, you could add a slice or two of deep-fried halloumi cheese. Or add a handful of freshly chopped mint and serve as a side dish with lamb. Add some lemon zest and serve with seafood and fish. If you have any leftovers, crumble in some feta cheese, stir in an egg, and pan-fry rice cakes in olive oil.

"Eating an artichoke
is like getting to know
someone really well."
Will Hastings

Anchovy and sage butter pasta

I like to fling this together with freshly cooked pasta when I am starving and need to eat in a hurry. I serve it with a huge bowl of fresh rocket, dressed with fresh lemon juice, extra virgin olive oil and Maldon salt, and topped with shaved Parmesan. There is nothing better than a big chunk of well-matured Parmesan cheese, with gorgeous big crunchy rock crystals in it.

- 150 g unsalted butter
- 8 fresh sage leaves
- 6 anchovy fillets
- 1 tablespoon capers
- ½ tablespoon green peppercorns in brine
- 2 cloves garlic, crushed
- 3 cups cooked pasta
- handful fresh Italian parsley, roughly chopped

Melt the butter in a frying pan and when it foams add the sage leaves. Cook them till they are crisp; remove and set aside.

Add the anchovies and stir them into the butter, mash them and then add the capers, peppercorns and garlic. Fling in the pasta and toss it well into the butter.

Stir in the parsley and sage, and then get down to the business of feeding that face. Enjoy!

SERVES 4

TIP: If you have a blob of creamy goat's cheese handy, stir that in too. This butter is also to die for on a juicy, rare steak.

When making a salad I love to mix the textures; it makes for a far more interesting dish.

Chicken noodle salad with a peanut dressing

THE SALAD
- 2 roasted chicken breasts, shredded
- 1 red pepper, cut into thin strips
- 4 spring onions with tops, sliced very thinly at an angle
- ½ English cucumber, seeds removed and cut into thin strips
- 1 peeled carrot, cut into matchsticks
- 1 very ripe sweet pineapple, peeled and cut into chunks
- ½ cup roasted cashew nuts, roughly chopped
- ½ cup toasted peanuts
- 2 cm fresh ginger, peeled and very finely shredded
- 1 red chilli, seeded and diced
- 1 cup cooked instant Chinese noodles
- ½ cup roughly chopped coriander
- ½ cup torn fresh basil
- 2 tablespoons roughly chopped fresh mint

DRESS IT UP
- 1 small chilli
- 2 cloves garlic
- 1 tablespoon palm or brown sugar
- 2 tablespoons fish sauce
- 2 tablespoons crunchy peanut butter
- 10 ml sesame oil
- ¾ cup lime juice
- ½ cup coconut milk

Toss all the salad ingredients together in a large bowl.

Fling all the dressing ingredients together in a liquidiser and give it a good whizz. Taste and adjust the seasoning; you might like it to have more fish sauce, or sugar or even peanut butter.

Pour the dressing over the salad and give it a good toss. Tip the salad out onto a serving platter and serve right away.

SERVES 4 – 6

76

Chicken cannelloni with homemade tomato sauce and a goat's cheese custard

I know that this recipe looks long and complicated, but I can assure you that it is not at all difficult to make and it is well worth the effort!

THE TOMATO SAUCE

- olive oil, for frying
- 1 large onion, finely chopped
- 2 cloves garlic, chopped
- 1 chilli (optional)
- 2 sticks celery, finely chopped
- 2 x 400 g canned tomatoes with their juice
- ½ glass red wine
- pinch of sugar
- 2 teaspoons fresh thyme leaves
- salt and pepper
- 2 sage leaves, thinly sliced
- small pinch cinnamon
- 1 small clove garlic, crushed

Make the tomato sauce first. Heat a little olive oil in a saucepan and gently fry the onions, garlic, chilli and celery till they are translucent. (Keep some of the celery leaves aside to chop into the sauce at the end.) Add the tomatoes and cook gently till the tomatoes are cooked down. Add the red wine and simmer for 5 minutes, and add a pinch of sugar to balance the dish.

Stir in the fresh thyme and cook for a further 5 minutes. Taste the sauce and adjust the seasoning, then add the sage, cinnamon and extra garlic. Add the celery leaves now, not too much!

Cook for 10 minutes more, on simmer; then set aside.

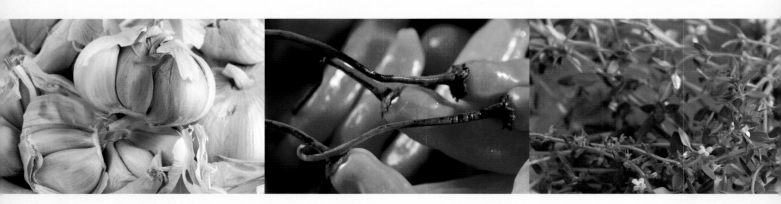

THE CANNELLONI

- 12 sheets homemade cannelloni, or bought lasagne sheets
- 1 large bunch fresh spinach
- 4 large leeks, white part only
- 50 g unsalted butter
- 4 cloves garlic, chopped
- 200 g chicken breast fillets, sliced and seasoned
- salt
- freshly ground black pepper
- 1 cup fresh ricotta cheese
- ½ cup hard goat's cheese, grated

THE CUSTARD

- 50 g Fairview Chevin
- 2 eggs, beaten
- 1 cup fresh cream
- salt and pepper, to taste

Now prepare the cannelloni. Wash the spinach and leeks well. Cut the stalks out of the spinach. Keep half of them and slice them thinly. Shred the spinach leaves roughly and blanch; squeeze out any water and drain them till needed.

Slice the leeks into thin rings, heat the butter in a saucepan and cook the leeks gently with the garlic. Add the spinach stems and chicken pieces, and cook till the chicken is just cooked through. Add the shredded spinach leaves and mix well.

Pop some of the chicken mix into your mouth and taste to see if it needs more seasoning, and then set it aside to cool down. Then add the ricotta and goat's cheese to the mixture, and stir it in well.

Lay the sheets of pasta onto a lightly floured work surface. Divide the chicken mixture into 12. Place a portion of the chicken mixture onto a sheet of pasta lengthways, leaving a 1 cm border from the side closest to you. Roll up and seal with beaten egg.

Place seam-side down into a baking dish, and cover with the tomato sauce. Beat all the custard ingredients together and pour over the pasta.

Bake at 180 °C for about 30 minutes till the top is golden and bubbling. Serve with a crunchy green salad.

SERVES 6

TIP: 12 rolled-up cannelloni will usually fit into the average oven-proof dish.

Aubergine and butternut lasagne

THE LASAGNE

- 1 medium, long-necked butternut
- olive oil
- brown sugar
- salt
- fresh rosemary
- 3 long, firm aubergines
- 1 kg cherry tomatoes
- 4 roasted red peppers, peeled and sliced
- 10 blanched spinach leaves, chopped
- 4 tablespoons basil pesto
- 8 cooked lasagne sheets
- 150 g mozzarella balls, torn
- 100 g grated Parmesan cheese
- 2 large tomatoes, sliced
- salt, to taste
- freshly ground black pepper

THE WHITE SAUCE

- 500 ml warm milk
- 1 fresh or dried bay leaf
- 2 tablespoons butter
- 2 tablespoons flour
- salt and pepper, to taste
- freshly grated nutmeg, to taste

Peel and chop the butternut into chunks. Toss in some olive oil, sprinkle with a little brown sugar and salt, and add a few fresh rosemary needles. Roast at 180 °C till just done.

Slice the aubergines quite thickly; salt them and let them drain for 20 minutes. Give them a quick rinse and pat them dry, then drizzle with a little olive oil and grill till cooked.

Remove the stems from the tomatoes and drizzle with olive oil and add a pinch of salt. Roast at 180 °C till wrinkly, and make sure to keep the juices.

While the tomatoes are roasting, make the white sauce. Heat the milk gently in a small saucepan with the bay leaf. Set it aside, and let the flavour infuse for a few minutes. Strain before using.

Melt the butter in a heavy-based saucepan then mix in the flour off the heat until smooth. Return to the stove and stir continuously over gentle heat till it thickens to a paste; do not allow the roux to brown.

Remove the saucepan from the heat, and slowly add the strained, warm milk, stirring continuously till thoroughly blended. Back on the stove it goes; bring to boiling point, then simmer gently for about 5 minutes until the sauce is smooth and creamy. Keep stirring!

Remove from the heat one last time, and season with salt and pepper, and freshly grated nutmeg. Set aside.

Keep the oven at 180 °C. Line a rectangular baking dish with half the vegetables and basil pesto, cover with half of the white sauce, and sprinkle with half the Parmesan cheese.

Cover this with 4 sheets of cooked lasagne and top with the remaining vegetables and white sauce. Sprinkle over the rest of the Parmesan cheese and top with remaining lasagne sheets. Finish off with the mozzarella and the sliced tomatoes, seasoned with salt and pepper.

Bake for about 20 minutes, or until the pasta is heated through and the cheese is bubbling and golden.

SERVES 4 – 6

Smothered salmon pasta

- 2 tablespoons butter
- 3 cloves garlic, finely chopped
- 4 spring onions with tops, chopped
- 250 g cream cheese
- 250 ml cream
- 250 ml milk
- 1 tablespoon creamed wholegrain mustard
- 200 g smoked salmon, chopped
- 200 g Norwegian salmon, diced
- 3 tablespoons roughly chopped fresh dill
- 3 tablespoons roughly chopped fresh chives
- 2 teaspoons fresh lemon zest
- salt
- freshly ground black pepper
- 1 small red chilli, chopped (optional)
- 400 g ready-cooked tagliatelle, kept warm
- 2 tablespoons finely grated Parmesan cheese (optional)
- 2 tablespoons deep-fried capers, chopped

This is a quick and easy dish to prepare for a houseful of hungry, impatient boys!

Heat the butter in a medium-sized saucepan and add the garlic and spring onions. Cook, stirring till the garlic becomes fragrant. Now stir in the cream cheese, cream and milk, and let it simmer for 5 minutes.

Stir in the mustard, both lots of salmon, herbs and zest. Season with salt, pepper and chilli, and bring to a simmer. Stir into the cooked pasta.

Serve in bowls and dust with Parmesan and chopped capers. Delicious!

SERVES 4

"The most indispensible ingredient of all good home cooking: love for those you are cooking for."
Sophia Loren

Seafood pasta

There is nothing more satisfying or tasty than a seafood pasta.

- 2 tablespoons olive oil
- 2 leeks, white part only, thinly sliced
- 2 sticks celery, chopped
- 1 large red pepper, finely chopped
- 4 cloves garlic, crushed
- 1 tablespoon tomato purée
- 1 teaspoon sugar
- 500 g fresh tomatoes, finely chopped
- ½ cup white wine
- salt
- freshly ground black pepper
- 1 packet seafood mix
- 20 fresh basil leaves, torn or roughly chopped
- ½ cup freshly chopped parsley
- 2 teaspoons fresh lemon zest
- 400 g linguine or spaghetti

Heat the olive oil in a large saucepan. Add the leeks, celery, red pepper and garlic, and cook till wilted. Add the tomato purée, sugar, chopped tomatoes and wine, and season with salt and pepper.

Cook the sauce till it starts to reduce, then add the seafood mix and cook very slowly for 10 minutes. Do not allow the sauce to boil rapidly; you want to keep the seafood soft and succulent, and coax out all the delicious flavour it has to offer.

In the meantime, cook the pasta according to the instructions on the package; do not over-cook!

Remove the sauce from the heat, and stir in the herbs and lemon zest. Add the cooked pasta and stir together gently to coat.

SERVING TIPS: Pile into a bowl and serve with a fresh green salad of mixed crunchy leaves, lightly tossed in lemon vinaigrette and topped with shaved Parmesan. You can also serve this as a seafood stew on basmati rice, by stirring hake chunks into the sauce near the end of the cooking time.

SERVES 6

TIP: Never cook a seafood mix on a high, rapid heat as it causes the tender, delicate flesh to toughen and become very chewy. So rather be patient and enjoy the results of your efforts!

This is one of my favourite sauces; it's chunky and delicious stirred through angel hair pasta or served layered under sheets of pasta for a dinner party. Caress anything with a blanket of this delicious sauce.

Smoked salmon and asparagus pasta parcels

- 250 g fresh green asparagus
- 400 g smoked salmon
- 1 tablespoon butter
- 2 cloves garlic, crushed
- 1 tablespoon green peppercorns in brine
- 2 cups fresh cream
- 1 tablespoon chopped fresh dill
- 1 tablespoon capers
- 4 spring onions with tops, thinly sliced
- 8 sheets of cooked lasagne
- freshly grated Parmesan cheese (optional)

Lightly steam the asparagus and drain. I'm watching you, don't over-cook them now! Divide into 8 portions and set aside. Divide the salmon into 8 portions and set aside with the asparagus.

Heat the butter gently and add the garlic and green peppercorns. Cook for a minute or so, then add the cream and cook till the mixture is reduced by a third. Stir in the dill, capers and spring onions, and remove from the heat.

Now let's put the parcels together. Lay the pasta sheets out on a flat surface and in the centre of each sheet place the asparagus and top with smoked salmon. Spoon over some sauce, roll the parcels up, place onto 4 hot plates (allowing two per person) and top with the remaining sauce.

Dust with freshly grated Parmesan cheese, serve with fresh lemon wedges, a huge green salad and a really chilled glass of what you fancy, and eat instantly.

SERVES 4

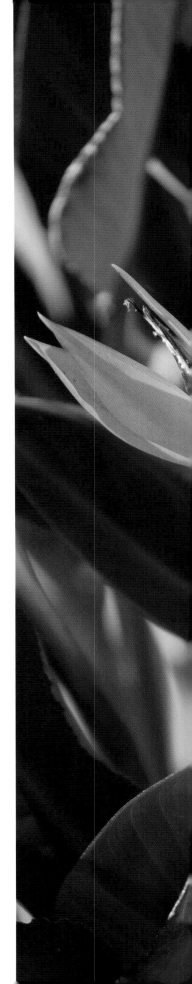

CHAPTER FIVE

Just *Kidding!*

When we were children, Mom would tell us all the usual fairy tales, like 'The Seven Little Goats', 'Little Red Riding Hood' and so on, but the ones I enjoyed the most were the ones she told about her own childhood and the gardens where she herself had grown up.

After Sunday lunch we would go out into our magnificent garden with its rockeries overflowing with portulaca, hedges full of roses and granadillas, and dahlias as big as fish plates, and she would tell me about her mother's garden.

To the side of the house was a huge old oak tree with big shady branches that seemed to spread out forever. My grandmother would hang pots from the branches filled with moss, maidenhair ferns and flowers, even strawberries; it was home to all kinds of plants. I'd love to have a tree like that in my garden.

Everything my grandmother planted flourished. And I can tell you now, my mother inherited her green fingers, which she passed on to me, and my brother and sister.

I am thanking God for those green fingers!

Nannygoats

Origen	: Switzerland
White	: Saanen
Black / White	: Alpine
Feed	: Complete feed
	: Lusernhay
	: Concentrate
Lifecycle	: Serve March / April
	: Kid Aug / Sept
	: Kids weaned after 5 days
	normaly twins
Lactation period	: 300 days
	65 days dry

"There's always free cheese in a mousetrap."
Unknown

More and more people are making their acquaintance with goat's cheese these days and just loving it. I'm not kidding! It comes in different shapes, sizes and textures; one of my favourite versions is the soft, silky chevin made locally by Fairview Estate.

Goat's cheese has a tangy flavour and can be distinguished quite easily from cheese made from cow's milk. There are times when the taste can be quite strong and some people just don't like it – they say it is 'goaty'. But I urge you to give it a chance; it will grow on you and you may just come to love it!

So many people nowadays suffer from lactose intolerance, a condition that makes it difficult to digest the lactose contained in cow's milk and cheese. The good news is that some lactose-intolerant people are able to cope quite comfortably with goat's cheese; the fat molecules are shorter than those found in cow's milk, making them more digestible. Goat's cheese is also a good source of bone-preserving calcium and is lower in calories than its cow's milk counterpart.

Little goat's cheese parcels

THE FILLING
- 250 g Fairview Chevin
- 4 tablespoons flat leaf parsley, chopped
- 1 tablespoon fresh mint, chopped
- ½ cup chopped green olives
- 2 cloves garlic, crushed
- 1 potato, cooked and cubed
- 4 tablespoons cooked lentils
- salt and pepper, to taste
- 1 spring onion with top, finely chopped

FOR THE WRAPPER
- 30 wonton wrappers
- 1 egg white, lightly beaten
- oil for deep frying

Mix all the filling ingredients together and set aside.

Lay the wonton wrappers onto a flat work surface in a diamond shape; one point faces you and the other the wall or window. Divide the filling up so that each parcel has 2 teaspoons of the goat's cheese mixture. Keep the wrappers covered with a clean, damp tea towel (they dry out fast).

Place 2 teaspoons of filling in the middle of the wrapper, brush egg white around the edges, making sure that you wet all four sides (beat another egg white if you run out).

Lift the top and bottom edges of the wonton. Press them together firmly from the top to about halfway down to seal. Now bring together the left and right edges. Twist together, sealing the edges and forming a square pouch. Continue to fill the remaining wrappers.

Get your oil heated in a pan suitable for deep frying, drop in a cube of bread to test the heat; it should turn golden brown when the oil is ready. Cook the parcels a few at a time till golden. Drain on paper towels.

Serve warm with a large green salad of mixed leaves and lots of ripe, firm Rosa tomatoes.

SERVES 6

Sun-ripe tomato and goat's cheese salad

Serve this salad with some slabs of freshly grilled ciabatta bread, glistening with extra virgin olive oil.

- a healthy handful of fresh, wild rocket
- 4 firm, really ripe tomatoes, sliced
- zest of 1 fresh lemon
- salt
- freshly ground black pepper
- 200 g Fairview Chevin
- 1 tablespoon snipped chives
- extra virgin olive oil, for drizzling

Place the rocket onto a platter. Arrange the tomatoes over the top, and sprinkle with the lemon zest, salt and freshly ground black pepper.

Slice the goat's cheese onto the tomatoes, sprinkle with chives and drizzle with olive oil. Serve with a little squeeze of fresh lemon juice.

SERVES 4 AS A LIGHT LUNCH

Baked artichoke bottoms with goat's cheese, anchovies, pine nuts and thyme

This wonderfully rich and delicious light lunch appeals to all my senses. You will have your guests scraping their plates and licking their lips with pleasure!

- 12 canned artichoke bottoms
- 12 tablespoons Fairview Chevin
- 4 teaspoons fresh thyme leaves
- 2 tablespoons pine nuts, toasted
- freshly ground black pepper
- 12 small anchovy fillets
- really good extra virgin olive oil, for drizzling

Drain the artichoke bottoms well. Gently mix the goat's cheese with the thyme, pine nuts and freshly ground black pepper to taste.

Spoon the goat's cheese mixture into the artichoke bottoms – roughly, don't press it all down; that doesn't look very sexy!

Top each artichoke with an anchovy, give them a light drizzle of olive oil and then place onto an oven tray. Grill under a hot grill till the cheese takes on some colour. Don't burn them now!

Remove from the oven, place onto a platter and drizzle with lots of extra virgin olive oil. Serve with chunks of crusty sour dough bread and a huge salad of fresh rocket and cos lettuce, with masses of thinly sliced red onions.

SERVES 6

TIP: You can substitute some bacon for the anchovy fillets, if you prefer.

> "Lying there, I heard the gentle, drowsy tinkling of a goat-bell, and presently the herds wandered past us, pausing to stare with vacant yellow eyes, bleat sneeringly, and then move on."
>
> *Gerald Durrell in 'My Family and Other Animals'*

Potato and goat's cheese melts

SOMETHING SAUCY

- 1 tablespoon runny honey
- juice of 2 fresh lemons
- 2 tablespoons chopped mint
- ¾ cup olive oil

POTATO CAKES

- 500 g potatoes, peeled and coarsely grated
- 1 teaspoon cumin seeds, toasted and bashed
- 3 cloves garlic, crushed
- 5 spring onions with tops, sliced
- salt and black pepper
- 2 beaten eggs
- 1 small green chilli, sliced (optional)
- olive oil and unsalted butter for frying
- 300 g Fairview Chevin
- 300 g wild rocket, washed

These are delicious dressed with a lemon minted sauce.

Make the minted sauce first. Whisk all the ingredients together, taste and adjust seasoning. Allow the sauce to rest for 2 hours for the flavours to infuse.

Now make the potato cakes. Squeeze the liquid from the potatoes; mix in the cumin, garlic, spring onions, salt and pepper, eggs and chilli. Divide the mixture into 8.

Heat some oil and butter in a large frying pan, and cook the potato cakes a few at a time, pressing down firmly in the pan. Cook till nicely golden on one side, turn and cook the other side till golden. Drain on some paper towels.

Place the potato cakes onto a baking tray, top each one with goat's cheese and grill till the cheese is golden. Serve on a mound of wild rocket and dress with the minted sauce.

SERVES 4

TIP: Don't turn the potato cakes over till they are ready to let you do it, otherwise they will break!

Pear, bacon, goat's cheese and baby spinach salad

THE DRESSING
- ⅓ cup fresh lemon juice
- 1 teaspoon English mustard
- honey, to taste
- 2 cloves garlic, crushed
- zest of 1 lemon
- salt, to taste
- freshly ground black pepper
- ⅔ cup olive oil

THE SALAD
- 1 tablespoon olive oil
- 4 pears, peeled and cut into 8ths lengthways
- 250 g streaky bacon, crisply cooked and chopped
- 500 g baby spinach
- 300 g goat's cheese
- 1 small red onion, thinly sliced
- 2 teaspoons poppy seeds, toasted

Delicious fruity pears, salty bacon and goat's cheese; I just love it!

It's a good idea to make the dressing first; then you can serve your salad the minute it is ready. Mix all the dressing ingredients together, except the olive oil, and taste that it is to your liking – maybe more lemon juice or honey? When you are happy, add the olive oil and shake it up baby.

Now, make the salad. Heat the olive oil in a non-stick frying pan, and gently cook the pears till they take on a little colour. Do not over-cook; we need to keep the texture.

Toss together the bacon and spinach, and arrange on a platter. Arrange the pears onto that, blob on the goat's cheese and scatter with the onion rings.

Sprinkle with the poppy seeds and dress the salad just before eating.

SERVES 4 – 6

Plump chicken thighs kept moist and succulent under layers of potatoes, aubergine and tomato sauce, finished off with a creamy goat's cheese custard.

Aubergine and chicken bake topped with goat's cheese custard

THE TOMATO SAUCE
see page 78

THE CHICKEN
- 12 deboned chicken thighs, with skin on
- salt
- freshly ground pepper
- olive oil
- 2 onions, peeled and sliced into rings
- 6 cloves garlic, crushed
- 3 tablespoons fresh thyme leaves
- ½ glass dry white wine
- 4 aubergines, thinly sliced lengthways and lightly salted
- 6 parboiled potatoes

THE CUSTARD
- 2 cups fresh cream
- 4 eggs, beaten
- 400 g soft goat's cheese
- salt
- freshly ground black pepper

Make the tomato sauce first according to the recipe on page 78 and while it is simmering, get going on the chicken. Season those thighs with salt and pepper. Heat the olive oil in a large saucepan and brown the chicken thighs in batches.

To the same pan add the onions, garlic and thyme, and cook gently till golden. Add the white wine and cook for 1 minute.

Preheat the oven to 180 °C. Rinse the aubergine slices and pat dry. Pan-fry on one side in a little hot oil until tender and just starting to colour. Don't crowd the pan; fry in batches.

Peel the parboiled potatoes and slice them thinly, and arrange a layer of potato on the bottom of an oven-proof baking dish. Top with the chicken thighs and the cooking juices, and onto the thighs goes the onion mix. Arrange half the aubergine slices on top of that.

Now spoon over a layer of tomato sauce, then layer the remaining potatoes, followed by some more tomato, and finally the rest of the aubergine slices. Spoon the rest of the tomato sauce over the top.

Make the cheese custard by beating all the ingredients together well. Pour over the top of the dish and bake at 180 °C till puffed up and golden.

SERVES 6

Fresh ripe apricot, goat's cheese, rocket and red onion salad

- 300 g fresh rocket leaves
- 18 ripe but firm apricots
- 300 g Fairview Chevin
- 1 small red onion, very thinly sliced
- salt
- freshly ground black pepper
- Willow Creek lemon infused olive oil, for drizzling
- 1 teaspoon fresh thyme leaves, for scattering

Place the rocket onto a platter. Halve and stone the apricots (out with the pips, baby!) Place a blob of goat's cheese in the centre of each apricot half and arrange them on the rocket. Toss the onion rings over the apricots in an untidy fashion.

Season with salt and lots of freshly ground black pepper. Drizzle with lemon infused olive oil and scatter with the thyme leaves.

SERVES 4 – 6

TIP: Add a splash of fresh lemon juice if you like.

Goat's cheese and beetroot rounds

THE DRESSING
- 1 tablespoon fresh thyme leaves
- 1 clove garlic, crushed
- 2 teaspoons Dijon mustard
- 1 teaspoon honey
- 1 teaspoon fresh orange zest
- salt
- freshly ground black pepper
- ⅔ cup freshly squeezed orange juice
- 10 ml red wine vinegar
- ⅓ cup extra virgin olive oil

THE BEETROOT
- 4 medium-sized beetroot, roasted and peeled
- 120 g Fairview Chevin, divided into 4
- 3 tablespoons pine nuts, toasted
- salt and black pepper
- 200 g wild rocket
- 1 red onion, thinly sliced

When I prepare beetroot, I always leave the root attached to the beet and a short bit of the stem intact. This makes for delicious, juicy, jewelled beetroot – the colour and flavour do not bleed away when it cooks.

For the dressing, blitz all the ingredients together in a blender, taste and adjust the seasoning.

Trim the tops and bottoms of the beetroot, slice in half through the middle and then shape the chevin portions into patties the same size as the beetroot. Press the patties into the pine nuts and season them with salt and pepper.

Divide the rocket between 4 plates. Place the bottom half of the beetroot onto the rocket, top with a cheese patty and some onion rings, and spoon over some dressing. Then cover with the beetroot tops and spoon over some more dressing.

Serve with toasted ciabatta.

SERVES 4

CHAPTER SIX

Bold *Beginnings*

My father loved nothing more than fresh mussels picked straight off the rocks, and he taught us how to do that.

He would wake us up at the crack of dawn to go fishing at Umhlanga Rocks, and the only good thing about getting up at 4 am was the steaming hot cup of tea that came with it – my mom makes a great cup of tea.

The first thing he'd do when we got to the beach, after we'd unpacked everything (I often wondered why we needed half of it) was to get a fire going for the mussels, then get some water from the sea and put it in a big tin.

We'd pick oysters and mussels from the rocks, eating the oysters straight from their shells with nothing more than a splash of lemon juice. (We always brought some fresh lemons with us from our garden at home.) There was no Tabasco sauce in those days.

If it winked back at you, you knew the oyster was alive and it was safe to slurp it down.

Oysters dressed with fresh pomegranate juice

- 4 or 6 shucked and cleaned Knysna oysters per person

FOR THE DRESSING
- 1 cup freshly squeezed pomegranate juice
- 1 tablespoon extra virgin olive oil
- salt
- coarsely ground black pepper
- 1 teaspoon freshly grated lemon zest
- 1 red chilli, finely chopped
- 2 teaspoons finely chopped fresh coriander

An oyster should be so fresh that it says, 'Shuck me, suck me and swallow me whole'. This delicious dressing will have them licking their lips, and the oyster shells, with pleasure.

Mix the dressing and let it stand for 1 hour. Arrange the oysters on a pure white plate and spoon a little of the dressing over each one.

SERVES 4 – 6

TIP: This dressing is sufficient for 24 oysters. Fresh oysters spiked with tequila and fresh limes are also a treat!

Smoked salmon parcels

- ½ small English cucumber, peeled, seeded and diced
- 2 teaspoons fresh lime juice
- 2 teaspoons fresh dill, chopped
- 250 g cream cheese
- 1 tablespoon chopped capers
- 2 spring onions with tops, very thinly sliced
- 150 g smoked mackerel, flaked
- 8 slices of smoked salmon (about 400 g)
- fresh rocket and watercress, enough for 4 small salads

Mix together the cucumber, lime juice, dill, cream cheese, capers, spring onions and mackerel.

Line 4 ramekins with cling film, overlapping the sides. Now line each ramekin with 2 slices of the salmon, make sure that the ends overlap the edge of the ramekin, so that you can close up the filling.

Spoon the filling into the ramekins; press down and smooth it. (There is bound to be some filling left over, just eat it with toast the next day.) Fold over the overlapping ends of the salmon and pull over the overlapping cling film. Seal well and chill the parcels for 1 hour in the fridge.

Place the rocket and watercress onto individual plates. Open the parcels and use the ends of the cling film to remove them carefully from the ramekins. Place a parcel onto each of the salads, garnish with fresh lemon wedges, and serve with the most delicious bread you can find.

SERVES 4

Zesty lime-seared scallops

I just love a meaty scallop, lightly seared and tasting of itself.

- 24 scallops, with coral intact
- grated zest of 3 limes
- 1 teaspoon fish sauce
- ½ teaspoon sesame oil
- salt
- freshly ground black pepper
- 1 teaspoon finely grated ginger
- 1 teaspoon olive oil

Marinate the scallops in a bowl with the lime zest, fish sauce, sesame oil, salt, pepper and grated ginger. Toss the scallops in 1 teaspoon of olive oil and sear them, a few at a time, in a hot, non-stick pan. Serve on an avocado and spring onion salad, topped with a lime and chilli aïoli (see recipe on page 222).

SERVES 4

TIP: Squeeze the juice from the 3 limes and freeze till you can use it in a sauce, drink or dressing.

Fresh garden snails

Maria Marzio, a good family friend, used to plunder my garden for snails, and I let her until I got to taste what she did with them! Then we got Quack our pet duck who was wonderful with pest controlling our garden, but we were left without snails for the pot for about two years. Then Quack took off to find himself a wife – no, he never landed in my pot, although I did have obscene thoughts of dark, plump, juicy cherries, honey and soy sauce on some days when he bit me!

Before we even get started, it is most important that only fresh, live organic snails be used. If you have put snail bait down, don't even consider using them – you will just die!

You will need:
- a very large pot with a tight-fitting lid
- maize meal or coarse polenta
- lots of garden snails that fit the criteria

Give the snails a little shower to get rid of any visible dirt; don't soak them in water! Place a layer of maize meal in the bottom of the pot. Take care not to overcrowd the pot; rather use two pots if necessary as we want healthy snails. The snails eat the maize meal and will purge themselves in the process. Keep changing the maize meal every day for about three days. Discard any dead snails!

On the fourth day, remove the snails and put them into the sink; sprinkle them liberally with salt. The snails will start to foam and give off their slime. Rinse them well in cold running water.

Boil a large pot of water with 1 cup of vinegar. Add the snails in batches and cook them for about 7 minutes; remove and continue to cook the rest. When they are all cooked, remove them from their shells.

Serve with garlic and parsley butter or in a rich garlicky, wine-infused tomato sauce with lots of freshly chopped parsley. Make sure you have lots of whole-wheat bread for mopping up those buttery garlic juices!

If you have gone mad collecting snails, freeze some in an airtight container to serve with a sauce of your choice; lovely with creamy polenta!

Butter bean pâté

- 2 cans butter beans, drained and rinsed
- 1 tub smooth cottage cheese
- 2 cloves garlic, crushed
- zest of 1 fresh lemon
- 1 tablespoon chopped fresh mint
- 1 tablespoon roughly chopped fresh coriander
- 1 small red chilli, finely chopped (optional)
- salt
- freshly ground black pepper
- juice of 1 lemon
- 2 tablespoons olive oil
- 1 tablespoon roughly chopped flat leaf parsley
- extra olive oil, for drizzling
- smoked paprika, for dusting

This is a great starter served with a platter of fresh vegetables, such as cucumber, celery, quartered red and yellow peppers, tomato and anything that takes your fancy really. But it is not complete without ciabatta, lightly grilled with olive oil. Everyone helps themselves and there will be much finger licking. This is best eaten a few hours after the ingredients have had time to get to know one another.

Mash the butter beans and stir them into the cream cheese with the garlic, lemon zest, mint, coriander and chilli. Season with salt and pepper, and stir in the lemon juice, olive oil and parsley.

Spoon the pâté into a bowl, drizzle with olive oil and give it a dusting of smoked paprika.

Add a few chopped anchovies, or stir in some chopped black olives, if you like.

SERVES 4 – 6

Iced tomato and vodka soup

- 300 ml fresh tomato juice
- 100 ml vodka
- juice of 2 ripe lemons
- zest of 1 ripe lemon
- 6 drops Worcestershire sauce
- 8 cubes cracked ice
- ½ green pepper, finely diced
- ½ celery stick, finely diced
- celery salt
- freshly ground black pepper
- 2 celery leaves, very finely sliced
- fresh basil leaves
- cucumber sticks
- Maldon salt flakes

Place the tomato juice, vodka, lemon juice, zest, Worcestershire sauce and ice in a blender, and blitz for a minute till well blended.

Pour into a freezer-proof dish, stir in the green pepper and celery, season with salt and pepper, and stir in the celery leaves. Freeze.

Once the mixture begins to freeze on the edges (after about 1 ½ hours), beat it with a fork and then freeze it again till it is nice and firm.

Remove from the freezer 30 minutes before serving and keep in the fridge. Spoon into glasses, top with basil, slide a cucumber stick in and sprinkle with a little Maldon salt. Serve with a spoon. Slurp and chew!

SERVES 6

The first time I ate ceviche was when I was on holiday in Mauritius. As I have a very adventurous palate and will try anything that won't bite me first, I was very excited to try this dish. I must say that the rest of the group looked on gingerly and wouldn't entertain the thought of raw fish back then; little did they know the fish was 'cooked' by the acid of the lime. The salad consisted of thin slices of freshly caught swordfish, thin rounds of calamari, sliced prawns, slithers of ginger, garlic, lime zest and juice, spring onions and coriander, with a little diced chilli and segments of lime.

Ceviche

- ½ English cucumber
- 300 g sashimi grade tuna, thinly sliced
- 200 g freshly shelled prawn meat, sliced in half
- 2 tubes cleaned calamari, very thinly sliced
- 1 red onion, thinly sliced
- 2 chillies, thinly sliced
- 1 teaspoon Maldon salt
- juice of 5 limes
- 3 tablespoons fresh coriander, plus extra for garnish
- 2 ripe avocado pears
- olive oil, for drizzling
- black pepper
- large bowl of butter lettuce

Using a potato peeler, slice the cucumber into long, thin ribbons; place the ribbons in the bottom of a flat dish. Lay the tuna, prawns and calamari rings onto the cucumber, top with the onion and chilli, and sprinkle the salt over that.

Pour on the lime juice and scatter with the fresh coriander. Swirl the dish to coat everything with the lime juice, cover and marinate in the fridge for 1 hour.

Check that the fish is opaque in colour; this means that the lime juice has 'cooked' it. If not, give it a swirl to cover with juice and leave to marinate until cured.

Peel and cube the avocados, toss them together with the ceviche, and pile onto a plate. Spoon over some of the lime juice, drizzle liberally with extra virgin olive oil, give it a good grind of black pepper and serve with a large bowl of butter lettuce.

SERVES 4 – 6

This is a nice dish to serve as a starter
or snack at your braai while the meat cooks. We love to
fill butter lettuce leaves with ceviche – roll them up and munch away!

Tomato jellies

THE TOPPING

- 1 teaspoon Worcestershire sauce
- 1 small red pepper, diced
- 1 fresh celery rib, thinly sliced
- 1 tablespoon chopped capers
- 1 tablespoon basil pesto
- ½ cup Rosa tomatoes, quartered
- 3 anchovy fillets, chopped
- 2 teaspoons lemon zest
- 2 spring onions with tops, thinly sliced

THE JELLY

- 15 g powdered gelatine
- 2 tablespoons freshly squeezed lemon juice
- 500 ml fresh tomato juice, heated
- 2 cloves garlic, crushed
- a dash of chilli sauce or Tabasco
- salt
- freshly ground black pepper

Lovely for summer – these tasty jellies can be made the day before.

Mix together the topping mixture, season to taste and spoon into the base of 8 small individual moulds.

Soften the gelatine in the lemon juice and add it to the heated tomato juice. Stir well until the gelatine has dissolved, then stir in the crushed garlic and Tabasco, and season with salt and pepper.

Spoon about half of the jelly mixture over the topping mix, and place the moulds in the fridge to set. Keep the rest of the jelly mixture out of the fridge – you don't want this to set just yet – reserving it for pouring over the moulds once they have set.

After about 2 hours, take the moulds out of the fridge; they should be partially set by now. Pour over the rest of the tomato jelly, and return to the fridge to set until firm.

SERVES 8

SERVING TIPS: Spoon over some sour cream and chives, and top with a few lightly steamed asparagus spears and some Parmesan shavings. Drizzle with olive oil and enjoy!

Caprese stacks

- 480 g cocktail tomatoes
- olive oil
- 480 g buffalo mozzarella (bocconcini)
- 150 ml basil pesto
- 8 large fresh basil leaves, for garnishing
- fresh cocktail tomatoes, for garnishing

SERVES 8

Switch the oven temperature onto full grill. Place the cocktail tomatoes on a roasting tray and drizzle with a little olive oil. Place them under the grill for 1 to 2 minutes, or just till the skin of the tomatoes starts bursting. Remove from the oven and cool.

Using 8 serving plates, place a tower mould onto each plate (you can use small tomato purée tins instead). Place a layer of roasted tomatoes on the bottom of each mould, top with mozzarella, then a teaspoon of basil pesto. Top with more tomatoes and more pesto, and place another layer of mozzarella onto the tomatoes. Press the filling down firmly into the mould and let it stand for 10 minutes.

When you are ready to serve, unmould the stacks by pressing down on the filling and lifting the mould gently. Garnish the top with fresh basil leaves and cherry tomatoes, and add a generous drizzle of extra virgin olive oil for good measure.

Sesame-seared tuna with wasabi sour cream dip

THE TUNA
- 2 small tuna loins
- 1 clove garlic, crushed and mashed to a paste
- 2 teaspoons sesame oil
- salt
- freshly ground black pepper
- 50 g white sesame seeds, toasted
- 50 g black sesame seeds, toasted
- olive or sunflower oil for searing the tuna

THE BIG DIPPER
- 1 cup sour cream
- 1 teaspoon fresh lemon zest
- salt
- 1 teaspoon chopped fresh coriander
- wasabi powder, to taste

Rub the tuna loins with the garlic paste and sesame oil, and season with salt and pepper. Mix the sesame seeds together and press the loins into the seeds, making sure that they are evenly coated.

Heat a non-stick frying pan with a little oil and sear the tuna on all sides, do not over-cook; this will take about 2 to 3 minutes.

When the tuna is cooked, cool it down and wrap each piece in tin foil, twisting the ends of the foil to form a cracker. Chill till you are ready to slice and serve.

Place all the dip ingredients, except the wasabi powder, into a bowl and mix together. Mix the wasabi powder with a little water and then stir it into the sour cream mixture; taste and adjust the seasoning.

When you are ready to serve, slice the tuna thinly and divide between 8 plates. Divide the wasabi dip between 8 small dipping bowls, give each guest a pair of chopsticks and tuck in!

SERVES 8

TIP: The tuna can also be served hot.

> "Never commit yourself to a cheese without having first examined it." *T.S. Eliot*

Deep-fried Camembert for the people

THE CHEESE
- 200 g Camembert cheese
- 3 tablespoons flour, or more if needed
- ¼ teaspoon smoked paprika
- salt
- freshly ground black pepper
- 2 large eggs, beaten
- 100 g fresh breadcrumbs
- oil for deep frying

TO SPOON OVER
- gooseberry jam
- sweet chilli jam
- fig jam
- cranberry jelly
- red currant jelly

This is a recipe my listeners on 567 Cape Talk radio have asked me for regularly over the last 14 years. Well, my darlings, this is for you!

Portion the Camembert into 8 wedges and place them in the freezer for 1 hour. Mix the flour with the paprika, salt and pepper. Roll the cheese in the flour, then dip into the beaten egg and coat evenly with the breadcrumbs.

Heat the oil, and test it with a cube of bread; it should brown in about 60 seconds. Now fry the Camembert till golden brown, drain on paper towels and serve with your favourite jam, some toasted ciabatta and a simple rocket salad.

SERVES 2

Hot mozzarella on ciabatta

THE CIABATTA
- 1 ciabatta loaf
- olive oil
- basil pesto
- cherry tomatoes

THE TOPPING
- 400 g mozzarella cheese, cut into cubes
- flour for dusting
- 1 cup buttermilk
- 2 cups fresh bread crumbs
- 1 tablespoon dried oregano
- ½ teaspoon celery salt
- 1 teaspoon smoked paprika
- oil for deep frying

Slice the ciabatta into thin slices, brush with olive oil and bake at 180 °C till crisp.

Dust the mozzarella cubes with flour, dip them into the buttermilk and then coat them with the breadcrumbs, herbs and seasoning. Chill the crumbed cubes in the fridge to set the crumbs; for about an hour.

Heat the oil in a saucepan and fry the cubes a few at a time till they are golden brown. Drain on paper towels.

Serve hot with the grilled ciabatta, pesto and tomatoes.

SERVES 4

The term 'panna cotta' is the Italian for cooked cream. Panna cotta is usually served as a dessert, made by simmering cream and sugar together, mixing it with gelatine, and then cooling it to set. This savoury version makes a superb starter.

Salmon and dill panna cotta

THE PANNA COTTA

- 1½ cups cream
- ½ teaspoon castor sugar
- 10 ml powdered gelatine
- 500 g natural Greek yoghurt

ROUGH STUFF

- 100 g chopped smoked salmon
- 2 tablespoons chopped dill
- 2 teaspoons ripe lemon zest
- 2 teaspoons lemon juice
- ⅓ cucumber, finely diced
- 50 g feta cheese, crumbled
- extra salmon for salmon roses

WASABI CREAM

- 1 teaspoon wasabi paste
- ¾ cup low fat natural yoghurt
- salt and pepper, to taste
- 1 tablespoon freshly squeezed lemon juice
- 2 tablespoons chopped chives

Make the panna cotta by placing the cream in a saucepan over a gentle heat; bring it slowly to the boil. Mix the gelatine with the castor sugar and stir into the hot cream until it has dissolved. Cool the cream and stir in the Greek yoghurt, then strain it through a sieve.

Mix the rough stuff together and stir it into the strained yoghurt mixture. Spoon the mixture into 6 ramekins and cover with cling film. Refrigerate until set. They can be made ahead and set overnight, or prepare them 3 hours before you want to use them.

Make the wasabi cream just before you are ready to serve. Mix all the ingredients together well.

To serve, dip the ramekins quickly in warm water to help unmould the panna cotta. Top the ramekin with the plate you are planning to serve it on and invert it – the panna cotta should slide out gently.

Top the panna cotta with some wasabi cream, a salmon rose and a small sprig of fresh dill. To make the salmon roses, simply roll a narrow strip of salmon up so that it resembles a 'rose'.

SERVES 6

CHAPTER SEVEN

Prawnography

On a visit to China with my friend Lynne Beckwith, we went to the market where they were just offloading a fresh delivery of dried baby shrimp. The Chinese use a lot of that kind of thing – dried scallops, calamari and a little fish that is similar to whitebait – to flavour food. When we saw these gorgeous pink things, there was no way we were going home without them, no matter what it took. I must have bought about 3 kg, and Lynne about the same, and we put them in our hand luggage.

We ran into a bit of trouble at the airport, being overweight as usual and having to try to explain the reason to the nasty little official behind the check-in counter. He eventually made us throw the shrimps out because they were stinking to high heaven by then!

Well, the one thing customs officials can't do is take away your food memories, or the recipes you have gleaned on your trip.

Peter's porky stuffed prawns with a honey-ginger dipping sauce

My friend Peter Currin is absolutely crazy about these stuffed prawns. They make him pant and flash his fabulous smile. A sensational starter served with different dips – this one's for you, Peter Pan!

THE PORK STUFFING

- 1½ cups pork or chicken mince
- 2 tablespoons chopped coriander
- 1 tablespoon chopped mint
- 1 tablespoon chopped dill
- 2 cloves garlic, crushed
- 2 teaspoons grated ginger
- 2 medium chillies, seeds removed and finely chopped
- 2 teaspoons lime zest (lemon will do)
- 1 teaspoon brown sugar or palm sugar
- 1 teaspoon fish sauce

DIPPING SAUCE

- ½ cup soy sauce
- 3 tablespoons black Chinese vinegar, or balsamic
- 1 tablespoon chopped ginger
- 2 cloves garlic, crushed
- 1 teaspoon sesame oil
- 1 tablespoon vegetable oil
- 2 teaspoons runny honey
- 1 red chilli, sliced
- 1 spring onion with tops, thinly sliced
- 1 tablespoon roughly chopped fresh coriander

THE PRAWNS

- 18 large tiger prawns
- cornflour
- 1 beaten egg
- 1½ - 2 cups fresh breadcrumbs
- oil for deep frying

Make the stuffing first by mixing all the ingredients well. Set it aside in the fridge until required.

Make the dipping sauce next. Place all the ingredients in a jar with a tight-fitting lid and give it a good shake. Let all those gorgeous flavours mingle while you prepare the prawns.

Remove the head and shells from the prawns, but leave the tail intact. Butterfly the prawns and remove the yucky, sandy vein.

Open each prawn out and place a tablespoon of the pork mix onto it; close it up again. Roll each prawn in a little cornflour, dip into the egg and coat in the crumbs. Chill in the fridge so that the crumbs can set.

Deep-fry until crisp and golden, drain on paper towels and serve with the dipping sauce.

SERVES 6 AS A STARTER

TIP: If you would rather not use crumbs, then you can cut strips of spring roll pastry and wrap them around the prawns, leaving the tails exposed.

This chapter is dedicated to my very precious friends, Alan Ford and Peter Currin, prawnographers of note.

The essence of a good dish lies in the ingredients; don't compromise on flavour and freshness. Respect your ingredients and the method in which they are prepared, and you will always serve meals that are tasty and nutritious. That's exactly what these boys do.

Watermelon sweetens on the plant, so once picked that is that – it doesn't sweeten further. My father would spend what felt like forever tapping watermelons for just the right hollow-sounding one, and that would be the one; ripe and ready, he would say! When choosing a watermelon, look for its G-spot, which is the creamy yellow patch under the melon that has been in touch with the earth while it has ripened in the sun. Or if you are into spanking, give it a few gentle taps – it should make a 'thunking' sound. Or do a little weight-lifting in the store; the watermelon should feel heavy.

Pink prawn and watermelon salad

THE SALAD
- 1 tablespoon olive oil
- juice of 1 lime
- salt
- 24 large shelled prawns, tails intact
- 3 cups cubed, firm watermelon flesh
- ½ cup shredded pickled ginger
- 1 clove garlic, crushed
- 2 spring onions, tops sliced at an angle
- 1 butter lettuce, washed, dried and leaves separated

DRESSING
- ½ cup good-quality mayonnaise
- 1 clove garlic, crushed
- juice of 1 lime
- ½ tablespoon chopped fresh coriander
- ½ teaspoon castor sugar
- 2 tablespoons olive oil
- salt
- freshly ground black pepper

Succulent firm steamed prawns, crispy and juicy watermelon, finished off with pickled ginger. After you have eaten it, you will feel like you are in the pink.

Mix together the olive oil, lime juice and salt, and drizzle over the prawns. Lightly steam the prawns till they turn pink; remove from the heat and set aside.

Make the dressing by whizzing everything together until well blended. Give it a taste and adjust the flavour.

Toss the prawns, melon, ginger, garlic and spring onion gently in the dressing. Place the butter lettuce onto a platter, pile the prawns on top of that, and enjoy.

SERVES 4

> "Watermelon – it's a good fruit. You eat, you drink, and you wash your face with it!"
> *Enrico Caruso*

Chilli prawns

Whenever I cook this dish it brings back wonderful memories of washing lines in the streets of Shanghai, with rings and rings of sausages pegged to them, drying in the wind!

- 24 large prawns
- 60 g unsalted butter
- 2 tablespoons olive oil
- 1 ring Chinese sausage, or chorizo sausage, cut into rounds
- 1 tablespoon chopped ginger
- 2 teaspoons peeled, chopped fresh garlic
- 6 large dried red chillies
- 1 tablespoon Chinese black vinegar
- 6 spring onions, thinly sliced
- 2 cups cooked rice
- 3 tablespoons chopped fresh coriander

De-poop the prawns, taking out the vein. Remove the shells but ensure that the tails stay on, and set aside.

Heat the butter and oil in a large pan and add the sausage, ginger, garlic and chillies. Cook for 5 minutes stirring all the time. When the sausage is nicely crisp, add the prawns and vinegar; stir around gently till they turn pink.

Remove the prawns from the pan and keep warm while you add the spring onions to the pan. Stir till they turn bright green then add the rice and heat through. Stir through the coriander.

Serve the prawns and rice with a wedge of freshly cut lemon and enjoy!

SERVES 4

Prawn balls

These make a delicious communal starter. Place a platter down on the table and let everyone spear the prawn balls on a skewer, dip and eat! This prawn mixture is also great for filling wonton wrappers – deep-fry then call them prawn cigars!

- 500 g prawn meat
- ½ cup chopped fresh coriander
- 2 teaspoons grated ginger
- 2 cloves chopped garlic
- 2 teaspoons fish sauce
- ⅓ cup cornflour
- 2 red chillies, chopped
- 1 spring onion with tops, finely chopped
- ½ cup fresh sweet corn kernels
- 2 egg whites, stiffly whipped
- oil for deep frying

Place the prawn meat in a food processor with the coriander, ginger, garlic, fish sauce, cornflour, chillies and spring onion, and blitz for 15 seconds to combine. Remove the prawn mixture from the processor and stir in the corn. Cook a spoonful to taste, and adjust the seasoning. Fold the whipped egg whites into the prawn mix – chill for 30 minutes.

Heat the oil and drop small spoonfuls of the mixture into the hot oil and cook till golden. Drain the prawn balls on paper towels.

Serve with a peanut sauce (see page 227) or sweet chilli sauce.

SERVES 4 AS A STARTER

Prawn and orange salad

There is nothing better than feeling the plump, firm texture of a fresh prawn in your mouth …

- 300 g cooked prawns
- 1 tablespoon fresh orange juice
- 6 ripe, firm oranges
- 2 peeled red onions, thinly sliced
- 2 red chillies, thinly sliced
- 2 tablespoons mint, roughly chopped
- 2 tablespoons coriander, roughly chopped
- 1 teaspoon cumin seeds, toasted

DRESSING
- zest of 1 fresh lime
- 2 cloves garlic, crushed
- ¾ cup freshly squeezed lime juice
- 2 tablespoons soft brown sugar
- 1 tablespoon sesame oil
- 1 tablespoon fish sauce

Remove the poop sac from the prawns but don't remove the shell – that's where the flavour is! Place in a large saucepan and splash with a tablespoon of fresh orange juice. Turn up the heat, and the minute the shells change colour to a beautiful bright orange, get them out of that pan, pronto!

Remove the shells from those plump little prawns, pop one into your mouth and savour that warm, firm flesh – you were going to steal one anyway! Place the remaining prawns in a dish.

Slice the oranges and toss them together with the remaining ingredients, using your hands, of course …

Now let's dress those naked, pink little prawn bodies. Shake together all the ingredients for the dressing until the sugar dissolves. Pour the dressing over the salad and give it a gentle toss – using your hands – so that all the good stuff gets mixed in.

Gently ease the salad onto a platter and serve.

SERVES 6

What is a poop sac?
The black vein that runs down the back of the prawn is its intestine, and is full of waste. To remove: make a shallow cut down the centre of the prawn's back and, using a toothpick, lift the vein and remove it.

Serve these seriously delicious cakes on a bed of fresh, minted cucumber ribbons anointed with sweet chilli syrup.

Sweet potato and prawn cakes

PRAWN CAKES
- 3 sweet potatoes peeled, cubed
- 300 g raw prawn meat, roughly chopped
- 3 cloves garlic, crushed
- 1 teaspoon grated fresh lime zest
- 1 fresh chilli, finely chopped
- ½ cup chopped coriander
- 5 spring onions with tops, finely sliced
- 1 cup toasted sesame seeds
- ¼ cup cornflour
- 2 eggs, beaten
- peanut or sunflower oil, for frying

SWEET CHILLI SYRUP
- 100 ml rice vinegar
- 100 ml white sugar
- 100 ml water
- 1 tablespoon thinly sliced ginger
- 3 red chillies, sliced
- 2 cloves garlic, thinly sliced

CUCUMBER RIBBONS
- ½ English cucumber
- a good handful of fresh mint
- olive oil
- freshly squeezed lemon juice

To make the prawn cakes, boil the sweet potato lightly and mash the cubes. Mix together with the prawn meat, garlic, lime zest, chilli, coriander and spring onions. Mould into 12 cakes.

Mix together the sesame seeds and cornflour. Dip each cake into the beaten egg and roll in the sesame seeds, coating well. Place the prawn cakes in the fridge to set for 1 hour.

In the meantime, make the sweet chilli syrup. Place all the ingredients for the syrup in a saucepan and boil till it has reduced by a third. The syrup should not be too thick; if it is reducing too fast, turn down the heat and add a little more rice vinegar. Cool and set aside till needed.

Using a potato peeler, slice the cucumber into long ribbons. Chop the mint finely and toss it through the cucumber ribbons with a little olive oil and freshly squeezed lemon juice.

Heat the oil in a large frying pan and fry the prawn cakes till golden; drain on paper towels.

Serve warm on minted cucumber ribbons, drizzled with sweet chilli syrup; serve some extra chilli syrup on the side if you like.

SERVES 4

I grew up with this wonderful, versatile vegetable growing in our back garden when I was a child. I never grow bored with it! In fact, I have chouchou growing in my garden for most of the year now and I often use it as a substitute for green papaya.

The pear-shaped chouchou, or chayote squash, originated in sub-tropical Central America and it now flourishes in hot regions all around the world. It grows on a vine and its firm, juicy flesh is very similar to that of a cucumber or marrow (in fact, these would both make good substitutes).

This delicious vegetable is just fabulous lightly steamed and lashed with olive oil and garlic – its mild flavour is perfect for pairing up with chillies, garlic and curry spices. It is also excellent eaten raw in salads or salsas, or marinated in lemon or lime juice. And it's good for you too – chouchou is rich in amino acids, potassium and vitamin C.

Chouchou salad with tiger prawns

This delicious salad can be made without the prawns – you can substitute green mango, or even add some green mango to it, if you like.

THE DRESSING
- 5 cloves fresh garlic
- 2 fresh red chillies
- 2 tablespoons palm sugar, or brown sugar
- 2 tablespoons fish sauce
- 4 fresh limes, juiced
- zest of 2 limes
- 2 tablespoons freshly chopped coriander
- ½ cup fresh mint leaves, roughly chopped

THE PRAWNS
- 16 large tiger prawns
- 2 tablespoons olive oil
- 4 cloves garlic, roughly chopped
- 1 teaspoon freshly chopped ginger
- Jenny Morris 'Chilli and Lemon Seasoning' (optional)
- ½ cup flat leaf parsley
- ½ cup fresh coriander
- juice of 1 very ripe lemon
- 50 g butter

THE SALAD
- 2 large chouchou, peeled and shredded

Make the dressing for the salad by pounding together all the ingredients, starting with the garlic, chillies and brown sugar. When these are almost smooth, stir in the fish sauce and the lime juice and zest. Taste and adjust the flavours; you might prefer more sugar or lime juice. Add the chopped herbs and stir them into the dressing. Set aside.

Clean the prawns, removing the vein but keeping the heads and shells intact, and butterfly them. Heat the oil in a large saucepan and place the prawns onto the base of the pan. Top with the garlic and ginger, and add a good shake of 'Chilli and Lemon Seasoning'. When the prawns turn orange on the bottom, flip them over and top with the herbs. Splash with the lemon juice and add the butter. When the whole prawn has changed colour, remove from the heat and serve immediately.

To serve, toss the dressing into the shredded chouchou and pile onto 4 clean white plates. Top each salad with 4 large prawns and serve immediately.

SERVES 4

"Would you like a prawn cocktail?"
"No thanks, I don't drink."
Jeff Stone

Asian prawn cocktail

I serve this dish either as a large salad for people to tuck into, or as individual starters. I use 'Chuck Me' which is one of my own products. It is sweet and slightly hot and really yummy. You can also use sweet chilli sauce, if you like.

- 800 g shelled, deveined prawn meat
- small bunch fresh coriander, roughly chopped
- ½ cup freshly chopped mint
- 2 spring onions with tops, thinly sliced
- 2 cloves garlic, grated
- ¾ cup homemade or really good bought mayonnaise
- ½ cup of Jenny Morris 'Chuck Me', or sweet chilli sauce

Place the prawn meat into a heat-proof bowl. Pour boiling water over the prawns and steep till they are pink and cooked.

Make the sauce by mixing the remaining ingredients together in a bowl. Pour the water off the prawns and while the meat is still warm, toss them into the sauce. Chill till you are ready to serve. Let them rest for at least 2 hours so that the flavours can develop.

Divide into 6 individual starter portions, or serve as a salad on a bed of fresh, young leaves. This also makes a mean prawn baguette!

SERVES 6

Noodle-wrapped prawn salad

This is a very impressive-looking starter. Your guests will give you a big pat on the back!

- 16 whole prawns, deveined
- 100 g egg noodles, soaked in water for 20 minutes
- oil for deep frying
- ¼ firm ripe avocado per person, thinly sliced
- 2 large carrots, shredded
- 1 cucumber, shredded into ribbons
- teriyaki sauce

Gently remove the shells from the prawns, keeping the head and tail intact. Divide the soaked noodles into 8 and wrap them around each prawn.

Heat the oil in a pot or deep fryer to a temperature of 170 °C, or until a cube of bread browns in about 30 seconds. Fry until the prawns are pink and the noodles are golden brown and crispy.

Place a ring mould onto a plate and layer the salad in the mould, starting with the avo, then the carrot and lastly the cucumber. Press down firmly and then remove the mould very carefully.

Thread 2 prawns onto a skewer and rest it on top of the salad tower. Drizzle with teriyaki sauce and serve.

SERVES 8 AS A STARTER

Green prawn rice

This makes a quick meal for unexpected guests, if you have prawn meat in your freezer.

- 100 g butter
- 4 cloves chopped garlic
- 4 spring onions with tops, chopped
- 1 large green chilli, chopped
- 500 g prawn meat
- juice of 1 ripe lemon
- zest of 1 ripe lemon
- ½ cup chopped dill
- ½ cup chopped coriander
- 2 cups cooked rice
- salt
- freshly ground black pepper

Heat the butter in a large non-stick frying pan. When the butter starts to foam, add the garlic, spring onion and chilli and cook for 1 minute.

Stir in the prawns and cook for 1 minute. Add the lemon juice and zest and half the herbs, and cook for 2 minutes. Stir in the rice, season, and heat through.

Stir in the other half of the herbs and serve with extra lemon wedges and a large green salad.

SERVES 4

CHAPTER EIGHT

Nothing *Fishy* about Fish

My father, bless his heart, was a keen fisherman and he would wake us up at the crack of dawn to go fishing. Thank goodness he'd load the car with all the heavy-duty gear the night before; all we had to do before leaving home was pick some lemons from the garden and pack the rustic loaves of *kuhne* bread and butter.

I love fishing, and my brother Billy and I learned how to bait our own hooks and how to cast at an early age. Someone would watch the rods; others would harvest the oysters and mussels, which we'd boil in a tin of seawater. Whatever fish we caught we'd gut and clean right there on the beach, but keep the scales so it stayed as fresh as possible until we got home to cook up a fishy storm.

As much as I whined about those early mornings, there was so much love and laughter at those breakfasts on the beach. Honestly, that tired heart of mine would melt the moment we ate.

I'd give anything to have those mornings back to share with my children, or to have my father teach my children how to fish.

Mexican fried fish on a guacamole bean salad

THE SALAD

- zest and juice of 2 fresh limes
- 3 tablespoons olive oil
- 1 medium red onion, chopped
- 4 firm ripe tomatoes, chopped
- ½ bunch roughly chopped coriander
- ½ cup chopped parsley
- 2 green chillies, chopped
- 1 x 400 g tin red kidney beans, drained and rinsed
- 1 tablespoon red wine vinegar
- salt
- freshly ground black pepper
- 2 firm, ripe avocado pears

THE FISH

- 800 g hake fillets, skin on
- 2 cups fine polenta
- ¾ cup cornflour
- salt and pepper
- 3 eggs, beaten
- oil for frying

Make the salad first and then fry the fish. Place all the salad ingredients, except the avocado pears, into a large bowl and gently mix together. Place in the fridge for an hour. Peel and dice the avocados at the last moment, and stir carefully into the salad just before serving.

To prepare the fish, mix together the polenta and cornflour, and season with salt and pepper. Dip the hake fillets in the beaten egg, then roll in the polenta and place in the fridge for 10 minutes.

Heat the oil in a non-stick frying pan and fry the fillets a few at a time till golden on both sides.

Serve with the guacamole bean salad and wedges of freshly cut lemon.

SERVES 4

How to choose a fresh fish

When you are buying fresh fish, you have to look deep into those little fish eyes; the eyes should be clear and bright and bulging, not jetlagged!

When you are holding that little fish head in your hands, check out the gills. They should be red and bright and almost bloody – give dull grey ones a miss.

When you run your fingers up and down that fish body, they should slide – the fish should feel slippery and moist – and the scales should be loose and moist, and not stick to the body. When you give the flesh a poke, make sure it is firm to the touch; steer clear of anything that is spongy or soggy and doesn't bounce back.

If the flesh smells fishy, don't take it. It should smell clean and fresh like the sea.

Yummy fish cakes with crushed caper and anchovy potatoes

FISH CAKES

- 500 g lightly steamed hake, flaked
- 2 cloves garlic, crushed
- 3 spring onions with tops, finely chopped
- ½ teaspoon grated fresh ginger
- zest of 1 small ripe lemon
- ½ teaspoon ground cumin
- ½ teaspoon ground coriander
- 1 cooked potato, mashed
- 1 small egg, beaten
- ½ cup chopped fresh coriander
- salt
- freshly ground black pepper
- oil, for frying
- flour, for dusting

POTATOES

- 4 tablespoons olive oil
- 2 cloves garlic, chopped
- ¾ cup roughly chopped green olives
- 1 tablespoon baby capers, liquid squeezed out
- 1 teaspoon finely chopped fresh rosemary
- 4 anchovy fillets, chopped
- 1 kg boiled baby potatoes
- 1 cup roughly chopped flat leaf parsley
- 50 g butter
- salt
- freshly ground black pepper

For me this is the perfect comfort food. I could spoon these delicious potatoes into my mouth the minute they are cooked; they are great served with all meats, fish and chicken.

To make the fish cakes, place the hake, garlic, spring onions, ginger, lemon zest, cumin, ground coriander, mashed potato, egg and fresh coriander in a bowl, and season with salt and pepper. Mix together well to incorporate all the ingredients. Let the mixture rest for 20 minutes before you cook a teaspoonful to check on the seasoning. Adjust the seasoning then shape into fish cakes.

While you are heating the oil, lightly dust the fish cakes with flour. Fry them in small batches till they are golden on both sides.

Now make the crushed potatoes. Heat the oil in a large non-stick pan, add the garlic, olives, capers and rosemary, and cook till it is aromatic. Stir in the anchovy fillets and potatoes. Crush the potatoes roughly, stir in the parsley and butter, and season with salt and freshly ground black pepper.

Serve with the fish cakes and a large green salad.

SERVES 4

On the days we didn't go fishing, my father would go down to the harbour at first light and buy fish. One morning I got up to have a bath and there was this huge snapper salmon, rock cod and grunter, all gasping for air in the bath. If only I had known about sushi back then. Can you imagine? Rock cod is now on the endangered list, so please don't eat it.

Steamed fish with a roasted pepper sauce

THE FISH

- 1 lemon, juiced
- salt
- freshly ground black pepper
- 2 cloves garlic, crushed
- 1 teaspoon dried oregano
- 1 tablespoon olive oil
- 4 x 300 g portions of firm white fish
- freshly chopped chives, to garnish

THE SAUCE

- 4 roasted red peppers, skinned
- 1 cup blanched almonds
- 3 large cloves garlic, peeled
- 1 small red onion, peeled and chopped
- 2 green chillies, chopped
- 2 fresh peeled ripe tomatoes, without pips
- 1 slice stale white bread without crusts, made into crumbs
- 2 tablespoons good red wine vinegar
- 6 tablespoons extra virgin olive oil
- zest of ½ lemon
- ½ teaspoon sweet smoked paprika
- salt and freshly ground black pepper, to taste

Mix together the lemon juice, salt and pepper to taste, garlic, oregano and olive oil. Rub all over the fish – back, front and sides. Steam the fish lightly and serve with the red pepper sauce.

Place the peppers, almonds, garlic, onion, chillies and tomatoes into a liquidiser and blend till smooth. Then add the breadcrumbs, vinegar, olive oil, lemon zest and smoked paprika. Zap it around till it is well mixed; season with salt and pepper.

Serve on a pile of crushed buttered potatoes, garnished with chives.

SERVES 4

Ricotta-stuffed salmon rolls

- 1 kg fresh Norwegian salmon, skin on

FOR THE STUFFING
- 1 tomato, skinned and diced
- 8 basil leaves, thinly sliced
- 2 tablespoons chopped dill
- 1 cup ricotta cheese
- 1 clove garlic, crushed
- salt
- freshly ground black pepper
- butter, for frying

LEMON CAPER BUTTER
- 2 tablespoons butter
- juice of 1 lemon
- 2 tablespoons capers

Cut 12 very thin diagonal slices from the salmon.

Mix the ingredients for the stuffing together. Lay the salmon out onto a flat surface and divide the stuffing between the slices. Roll up like little Swiss rolls, and chill in the fridge.

Heat some butter in a frying pan and cook the salmon rolls in small batches, just a few minutes each side, keeping them warm until they are all cooked.

To make the lemon caper butter, heat the butter in a small saucepan till it foams. Stir in the lemon juice and capers, and cook for 2 minutes. Drizzle over the salmon.

SERVES 4

TIP: Serve the salmon rolls with some creamy green onion mash (see page 210) and zesty green beans (see page 204).

Fennel, caper and orange salad with lightly steamed salmon

- fennel fronds
- 400 g Norwegian salmon
- olive oil
- 2 heads of fennel trimmed, washed and halved lengthways
- 2 small ripe lemons, juiced
- 5 tablespoons olive oil
- 1 tablespoon white wine vinegar
- 2 tablespoons capers
- 1 teaspoon roughly chopped fresh dill
- 2 oranges, peeled and pith free, thinly sliced
- 1 small red onion, thinly sliced
- salt and black pepper

Place a colander over a pot of simmering water, and place a few fennel fronds at the bottom of the colander. Lightly coat the salmon with a little olive oil and place it skin-side down onto the fennel. Steam for 8 minutes covered, or until it is only just cooked through. Cool the salmon and break into bite-sized chunks.

Slice the fennel heads into thin strips, place on a flat glass dish and sprinkle with a little salt.

Whisk together the lemon juice, olive oil and white wine vinegar.

Scatter the capers and dill over the sliced fennel, add the oranges and red onion, and season with a little salt and freshly ground black pepper. Add the dressing and mix together gently, using your hands, of course.

Scatter the salmon chunks over the salad, and serve immediately.

SERVES 4

"Fish, to taste right, must swim three times – in water, in butter, and in wine."
Polish proverb

These deliciously crisp little fish will rejuvenate your taste buds; eat the whole thing! All one needs to do to cook whitebait is to shake it about in a little seasoned flour and fry it quickly till golden and crisp. The entire fish is eaten. It is delicious served with large fresh wedges of lemon or with great blobs of flavoured butter, melting all over them.

Whitebait smothered with citrus chilli butter

WHITEBAIT
- 1 kg whitebait
- 1 cup flour
- salt
- smoked paprika
- black pepper

FLAVOURED BUTTER
- 250 g softened butter
- 2 cloves garlic, crushed
- 2 teaspoons fresh lemon zest
- 1 tablespoon finely chopped fresh parsley
- 1 small chilli, finely chopped (optional)
- 3 tablespoons fresh lemon juice
- salt and black pepper
- 1 teaspoon toasted cumin seeds, roughly ground

To prepare and cook the whitebait, defrost and drain them, then dab dry with a clean cloth. Mix the flour and seasoning together in a plastic bag. Shake the whitebait around in the bag until they are well coated with the seasoned flour. Deep-fry a few at a time till golden; drain and keep warm.

Stir all the ingredients for the flavoured butter together in a bowl and then spoon it into the dish you want to serve it in at the table.

Pile the warm whitebait onto a platter. Place a bowl of fresh lemon wedges, a fabulous green salad, crusty bread and the flavoured butter on the table and strike the dinner gong.

This whole meal is eaten with your hands; you are welcome to lick your fingers!

SERVES 4 – 6

TIP: I would serve this to 4 people as a light lunch or 6 as a starter.

"Fish should smell
like the ocean. If they
smell like fish, it's too late."
Unknown

Whole baby fish on wilted greens

FOR THE FISH
- 4 whole baby Cape salmon, cleaned and gutted
- 4 cloves garlic, peeled and sliced thinly
- zest of 2 unwaxed lemons
- 1 teaspoon ground Sichuan peppercorns
- 1 tablespoon finely chopped fresh coriander
- 1 small green chilli, finely chopped
- ¼ cup sesame oil
- juice of 2 freshly squeezed lemons
- 3 tablespoons olive oil

FOR THE GREEN THINGS
- 20 spring onions with tops intact, finely sliced
- 12 fresh green asparagus
- 3 heads of pak choi, sliced into 4 lengthways

Preheat the oven to 180 °C. Dry the fish well and make two slashes on either side of each fish. Set aside.

Place the garlic, lemon zest, Sichuan peppercorns, coriander, chilli and sesame oil in a blender and whizz to a paste.

Rub the fish with the lemon juice inside and out. Smear the paste into the slashes of each fish and set aside.

Heat the oil in a large frying pan, add the fish to the hot oil and fry for approximately 2 minutes per side.

Place the fish on an oven tray and bake for 10 minutes at 180 °C. Remove the tray from the oven and let it stand for 5 minutes while you wilt and plate your greens. Top the greens with the fish and garnish with a juicy wedge of fresh lemon.

SERVES 4

TIP: A blob of coriander butter to top the fish is what I like!

You can use any small fish for this, but bear in mind that if it is a bony fish you might like to get your fishmonger to butterfly them for you; not very sexy to sit at the table spitting fish bones into your hands, or worse still having someone choke on you. In my house they would have to die if the kids were not around, because I panic and run for the door with my hands over my face.

Hake with Portuguese-style olive and tomato sauce

- 3 tablespoons olive oil
- 2 bay leaves
- 3 whole cracked and finely bashed allspice berries
- 4 cloves garlic, finely chopped
- 1 green pepper, thinly sliced
- 1 onion, thinly sliced
- 2 medium, ripe tomatoes
- ½ cup dry white wine
- ½ cup small black pitted olives, rinsed
- 1 kg hake or other firm-fleshed white fish
- sea salt
- freshly ground black pepper
- freshly chopped parsley, for garnishing

Heat the olive oil in a frying pan and add the bay leaves; cook them for about 2 minutes or until they start to turn brown. The oil should be beautifully fragrant by now.

Now add the allspice and garlic, and give it a quick stir. Cook for about half a minute before adding the green pepper and onion. Then cook for about 5 minutes to wilt it down.

Peel and deseed the tomatoes, then slice into julienne strips. Add them to the pot and cook for a few minutes.

Add the white wine and olives; cook till the wine is slightly reduced. Taste, and season with salt and pepper.

Season the fish with salt and freshly ground black pepper. Lay the fish fillets onto the vegetables and gently cook through; remove from the heat.

Assemble onto a platter and spoon the sauce down the middle of the fish. Garnish with the parsley and drizzle with extra virgin olive oil. Serve with crushed parsley potatoes, a fresh green salad and Portuguese rolls to mop up the sauce.

SERVES 4

Seared tuna with a herby green bean purée

FOR THE BEAN PURÉE
- 400 g baby beans
- ½ tightly packed cup of fresh coriander
- ½ tightly packed cup of fresh Italian parsley
- 3 sprigs of fresh mint
- ½ teaspoon ground cumin
- 2 cloves fresh garlic, peeled
- zest of 2 lemons
- ½ cup olive oil
- 1 tablespoon capers
- 2 tablespoons toasted pine nuts

FOR THE TUNA STEAKS
- olive oil
- 4 tuna steaks, 200 g each
- sea salt and black pepper

Get a pot of salted water on a rolling boil, top and tail the beans and cook till just soft. While the beans are cooking, place the remaining purée ingredients into your blender.

Drain the beans and plunge them into a bowl of iced water to stop them cooking further, then drain and add them to the ingredients in the blender. Blitz till the mixture is smooth; taste and season with sea salt and freshly ground black pepper.

Rub a little olive oil onto both sides of the tuna steaks and season with sea salt and freshly ground black pepper. Heat a skillet and sear on both sides; don't over-cook!

To serve, place some bean purée on each plate and top with the hot, seared tuna and some lemon wedges.

SERVES 4

TIP: I don't add any lemon juice to the beans because it dulls the fresh green colour, but this purée does need some juice to lift it, so squeeze some on to taste!

I arrived in Durban in July 2005 to do a couple of food demonstrations. After picking up the rental car, I tuned the radio to the local music station and got lost in the wonderful oldies they were playing. The next thing I heard was a warning not to swim in the sea because of the sharks – there was a sardine run and the water was thick with jumping, jiving and thrashing little fish.

Memories of my childhood came flooding back – the frenzy of people on the beach, scooping up sardines.

My wonderful friend, Ruby Naidu, who feeds and spoils me and also taught me how to cook breyani, was not letting me go home without some of these rich, oily little fish. She cleaned and gutted two dozen, fresh from the sea, and presented them to me flash-frozen before I boarded my plane.

Ruby, this is how I cooked them!

Sardines for Ruby

- 24 fresh sardines
- ½ cup ground almonds
- 2 teaspoons orange zest
- 2 cloves garlic, crushed
- 1 cup day-old breadcrumbs
- 4 tablespoons candied orange peel, finely chopped
- 4 spring onions with tops, finely sliced
- 2 tablespoons Italian parsley, roughly chopped
- 1 tablespoon green olives, chopped
- juice of 1 lemon
- olive oil
- salt
- freshly ground black pepper

In loving memory of my Durban mother Ruby Naidu.

Preheat the oven to 180 °C. Clean and gut the sardines. Mix all the remaining ingredients together and divide into 24 portions.

Stuff the crumb mix into the belly of each sardine, and lay them out onto a roasting tray. Cut 2 slits into the top of each sardine and drizzle with olive oil. Season with salt and pepper. Bake in the preheated oven for 20 minutes.

Pack the sardines onto a platter with wedges of fresh lemon and get stuck in – put that knife and fork down!

SERVES 6

There is nothing to beat the flavour of fresh sole. I love the delicate, textured flesh but I am sad to say that so many millions of other people also do, and that is why there is a decline in the sole population. So I'm only going to eat sole four times a year to do my bit for a sustainable supply in the future!

My guilty sole

- 8 medium-sized soles, filleted

STUFFING
- ¾ cup fresh breadcrumbs
- 1 tablespoon lemon zest
- 2 tablespoons basil pesto
- 2 tablespoons olive oil
- salt, to taste
- black pepper

SAUCE
- 1 tablespoon olive oil
- 2 onions, chopped
- 2 stalks celery, chopped
- 3 cloves garlic, crushed
- 1 red pepper, diced
- 400 g can chopped tomatoes
- ½ cup pitted black olives
- 2 anchovy fillets, chopped
- 1 tablespoon fresh thyme leaves
- 1 tablespoon fresh parsley, chopped
- lemon wedges, to garnish

Mix all the ingredients for the stuffing together and set aside. Lay the sole fillets out on a flat surface and spread with the breadcrumb mix. Roll them up and pack them into an oven-proof dish large enough to hold them tightly. Preheat the oven to 180 °C.

In the meantime, prepare the sauce. Heat the oil in a saucepan and gently fry the onion, celery, garlic and red pepper, and cook for a further 5 minutes. Add the tomatoes and simmer for 10 minutes. Stir in the olives, anchovies, thyme and parsley.

Pour the sauce over the soles and bake in the oven for 15 to 20 minutes. Remove from the oven and let the dish rest for 10 minutes before serving.

Serve on creamy herbed mashed potatoes; pure comfort!

SERVES 4

TIP: If you are not sure if the fish you want to prepare is sustainable, SMS the name of the fish to 079 499 8795 and SASSI will advise. Eat responsibly. www.wwfsassi.co.za

Spicy baked fish

When I was about 12, I got a job in a fish and chip shop during the school holidays. I thought I was a really big deal because I introduced a few saleable products that they continued to sell until they eventually closed the business. Even then I knew without a doubt that I wanted to spend my life making people's taste buds happy!

- 3 tablespoons olive oil
- 1 large peeled onion, cut into thin rings
- 1 teaspoon cumin seeds
- ½ teaspoon fennel seeds
- 2.5 cm peeled ginger, finely chopped
- 4 cloves garlic, crushed
- ½ teaspoon ground turmeric
- 1 teaspoon ground coriander
- 2 large ripe tomatoes, grated
- 1 large red, 1 green and 1 yellow pepper, thinly sliced
- 2 green chillies, chopped
- salt, to taste
- freshly ground black pepper
- ½ cup roughly chopped coriander
- 1 kg firm white fish fillets
- 20 g butter

Heat the oil in a large frying pan and add the onions; cook gently for 5 minutes. Now add the cumin and fennel seeds and cook, stirring for 2 minutes.

Add the ginger and garlic and cook, stirring for 1 minute. Stir in the turmeric and ground coriander and cook for 3 minutes, adding a spoonful of water to stop the spices sticking.

Add the tomato and peppers, and simmer gently till the peppers are tender. Season with salt and pepper, and stir in the coriander. Remove from the stove and set aside.

Place the fish in an oven-proof dish and dot with a little butter. Spoon over the pepper mixture and bake at 180 °C for 20 minutes. Remove from the oven and let it rest for 10 minutes before serving.

Serve with crushed potatoes and a large mixed salad.

SERVES 4

Salmon carpaccio

- 400 g very fresh Norwegian salmon, very thinly sliced
- 1 tablespoon extra virgin olive oil, for frying
- 2 tablespoons baby capers
- 2 tablespoons extra virgin olive oil, for drizzling
- zest of 2 very ripe lemons, very finely shredded
- 1 tablespoon freshly chopped flat leaf parsley
- 120 g fresh wild rocket
- lemon wedges
- 2 ripe avocados
- fresh brown bread

Arrange the sliced salmon onto a white platter. Heat the oil in a frying pan and fry the capers until they are really crisp. Drizzle the olive oil onto the salmon and scatter over the lemon zest, parsley and capers.

Serve with a bowl of fresh wild rocket, lemon wedges, sliced avocado and freshly sliced farmhouse brown bread. This carpaccio is also delicious served with a wasabi dressing.

SERVES 4 – 6

TIP: If you place the salmon in the freezer and chill it for 15 minutes, it will be a lot easier to slice thinly.

The soft, gentle flavour of the leeks, the tart fresh lemon and the fragrant dill embrace the succulent salmon; I think it's a match made in heaven. I always cook salmon for the longest time on its skin-side to crisp it up; it is like yummy fish crackling. Eat the skin for goodness sake, just try it!

If you are like me, try adding another 200 g slice of salmon to your order, slice it thinly, give it a splash of soy sauce and eat it raw. Oh my goodness!

Buttered leeks, grilled salmon and creamy dill mash

- 1 kg young leeks, all white and pale green parts, sliced
- 100 g unsalted butter
- 3 cloves garlic, finely chopped
- 4 x 200 g fresh Norwegian salmon fillets, with skin on
- salt and freshly ground black pepper
- a little olive oil, for searing
- 100 ml fresh cream
- juice of 1 fresh lemon
- 1 tablespoon freshly chopped dill
- creamy mashed potatoes, to serve 4

Let's cook the leeks. I'm sure there is no need to tell you that the sliced leeks need to be well rinsed and dried. That done, time to heat half the butter in a pan and when it stops foaming, add the leeks and garlic. Cook gently, stirring, until they are tender. Do not brown them! Remove the pan from the heat and set aside till needed.

Time to season the salmon. The fillets should be firm and fresh; give them a good grind of black pepper and a little salt. In a clean, non-stick frying pan, heat a very small amount of oil and sear the salmon on both sides. Don't over-cook; you need about 2 minutes per side. Keep the salmon warm while you finish off the leeks.

Gently reheat the leeks, add the cream and lemon juice, and cook for about 3 minutes. Remove from the heat and stir in the remaining butter, a few small pieces at a time.

Stir the dill through the mashed potatoes and place a dollop onto a plate; top with leeks then the salmon. Garnish with a sprig of dill or a twist of fresh lemon.

SERVES 4

TIP: Whichever way you do it, try and get a bit of everything in your mouth at the same time!

Did you know?
Any fish is a source of good-quality protein, vitamins and minerals, but oily fish such as salmon also contains omega 3 fats that reduce blood clotting and inflammation.

CHAPTER NINE

Clucking or *Quacking?*

When last did your house or kitchen smell like home?

Those wonderful aromas that waft through the house from fresh bread baking in the oven. The smell of freshly chopped garlic and ginger as the hot oil releases its magic aroma into the room. The heady vapours that rise from a tomato sauce that has been allowed to bubble slowly on your stove or in a slow cooker, and the scent of tender fresh basil leaves crushed between your fingers to release their fragrance just before stirring them into a hot sauce.

Rosemary melting into a roasting chicken; buttery scones; cakes made with real vanilla; freshly tempered spices ground straight into the dish; the fragrance that wafts from a simmering pot – these are my treasured pleasures.

"If it looks like a duck, walks like a duck, talks like a duck, it probably needs a little more time in the microwave."
Lori Dowdy

"A good cook always
licks her fingers."
Unknown

My harissa buttered chicken

This delicious recipe is for my darling friend Naushad Khan. It makes enough harissa butter for 2 chickens – they are unbelievably moist and yummy from the butter, and the flavour just melts into the flesh.

HARISSA BUTTER

- 2 tablespoons toasted cumin seeds, roughly ground
- 1 teaspoon cinnamon
- 1 teaspoon paprika
- 10 cloves garlic, crushed
- 1 tablespoon grated fresh ginger
- 2 cups chopped fresh coriander
- large handful flat leaf parsley
- 1 whole preserved lemon with pulp
- 1 cup fresh rosemary needles
- 1 tablespoon Jenny Morris 'Chilli and Lemon Seasoning', or 3 fresh chopped chillies
- 3 tablespoons tomato paste
- ¾ cup fresh lemon juice
- 1 cup olive oil
- 300 g butter

FOR THE CHICKEN

- 2 big fat chickens, over 2 kg each if possible
- salt and pepper, to taste

Preheat the oven to 190 °C. Combine all the harissa butter ingredients in a food processor and blend until almost smooth.

Position the fat chicken on a clean flat surface; wiggle its legs, now push your fingers gently under the skin on the neck end and carefully work the skin away from the flesh. If you have short fingers, use the handle of a wooden spoon and gently lift the skin without poking holes in it! Once you have lifted the skin off the breast, gently work your fingers down to the thighs and lift the skin there.

Divide the harissa butter and push half of the butter under the skin. Position it onto the breast bone and then stroke it down to the thighs, and make sure you cover the breast as well. Rub your buttery hands all over the top and bottom of the chicken, and season with salt and pepper. Repeat the process with the second chicken, using the rest of the butter.

Roast the chicken at 190 °C till it is golden and crisp. (Roast your chicken for 15 to 20 minutes for every 400 g.) The legs should wiggle when you move them, and the juices run clear from the thickest part of the chicken.

Serve with a fruity couscous salad and lots of green leaves dressed with olive oil and fresh lemon juice.

SERVES 8 – 12

TIP: Please take the time to rest your chicken before you start to carve it. You will be rewarded with a juicy, succulent meal with all the flavour on your plate and not on the chopping board.

Orange chicken

I think chicken is delicious cooked with fruit, and oranges and chicken just love to be in each other's company!

- 100 g softened butter
- 2 cloves garlic, crushed
- zest and juice of 1 large orange
- zest of 1 lemon
- 1 red chilli, chopped
- 1 teaspoon salt
- black pepper
- 1 tablespoon fresh lemon thyme leaves
- 2 tablespoons chopped fresh parsley
- 1 x 2 kg whole chicken, or 2 smaller birds
- 4 large peeled potatoes, thickly sliced
- 2 peeled onions, sliced into rings
- smoked paprika

Preheat the oven to 200 °C. Mix the butter together with the garlic, citrus zest, orange juice, chilli, seasoning and herbs. Smear under the skin of the chicken.

Place the potatoes, onions and the chicken in a roasting pan. Rub a little more butter over the skin of the chicken, dust with some smoked paprika, and season with salt and pepper.

Roast at 200 °C for about 1 hour, or until the juices run clear from the chicken. Remove the chicken from the pan, return the pan to the oven and brown the potatoes for a few minutes.

Serve the chicken with the vegetables, taking care to scrape all the flavourful bits from the roasting pan.

SERVES 4 – 6

TIP: Once you have plundered the base of the roasting pan, pour in some hot water and scrape off whatever is left; spoon it into ice trays, freeze and use to enrich a gravy.

Lemon and rosemary thighs

These are delicious and I use the marinade on fish and lamb as well. You can braai or barbeque the chicken if you don't want to roast it.

- 12 deboned chicken thighs, with skin on

MARINADE
- 4 tablespoons olive oil
- 6 tablespoons lemon juice
- 3 tablespoons rosemary needles
- 1 fresh bay leaf, chopped
- 2 tablespoons chopped onion
- 3 cloves garlic, chopped
- 2 teaspoons lemon zest
- salt
- freshly ground black pepper

Place all the marinade ingredients in a blender and blitz till smooth. Place the thighs skin-side down in a flat dish and pour over the marinade, covering well. Marinate for 2 hours, turning from time to time.

Preheat the oven to 190 °C. Transfer the chicken to a roasting pan and roast till golden and cooked through; approximately 35 minutes. Baste with the left-over marinade every now and then.

Serve with a large crunchy mixed salad and crispy potato wedges.

SERVES 4

TIP: I like to put the thighs in a zip lock bag with the marinade – that way I don't have to turn them!

A few of my friends get freaked out when I say that I am cooking chicken with 40 cloves of garlic. Everyone has their own twist on this classic French dish and those of us who have had it before, know that when the garlic has cooked in its husk it is meltingly soft, mellow and mildly flavoured. I have to fight everyone off once they have had their first taste of this fragrant squishy garlic; you just squeeze it out of its skin onto your chicken and your mouth will be forever grateful!

40 Clove garlic chicken and butter beans

- 1 really large free-range chicken
- olive oil
- salt
- freshly ground black pepper
- 40 g unsalted butter
- 1 tablespoon olive oil
- 40 garlic cloves, in their skins
- 1 tablespoon fresh rosemary needles, finely chopped
- 2 bay leaves
- 3 sprigs thyme
- 1 large onion, thinly sliced
- 3 large potatoes, peeled and thinly sliced
- 3 cans butter beans, drained
- 1 cup sundried tomatoes roughly chopped
- 400 ml white wine
- 200 ml chicken stock

Get the oven on and preheat to 200 °C. Now oil the chicken with a little olive oil and season well with salt and freshly ground black pepper.

Heat the butter and olive oil in a heavy-based saucepan large enough to hold the chicken and vegetables. When the butter foams, add the chicken and brown it gently on all sides. Remove the chicken and add the garlic to the saucepan, stir frying for 1 minute. Add the rosemary, bay leaves, thyme and onion, and stir fry for 2 minutes.

Layer the potatoes onto the onions, and then the beans and sundried tomatoes. Add the wine and stock, and place the chicken onto that. Cover the saucepan with a couple of layers of foil and seal tightly.

Cook in the oven at 200 °C for an hour, then remove the foil and brown the chicken skin for about another 15 to 20 minutes.

Remove the chicken and vegetables from the roasting pan and pour off the sauce. If the sauce is too thin, simmer on the stove for about 10 minutes.

Carve the chicken after it has rested for 10 minutes and serve it on top of a pile of beans and potatoes with a really crisp green salad.

SERVES 4

"The rooster may rule the roost, but the hen rules the rooster." *Unknown*

Chicken pie

A quick, cheat's way to fling together a saucy pie to serve with a huge green salad.

- 3 tablespoons butter
- 1 large onion, finely chopped
- 4 cloves garlic, chopped
- 1 punnet button mushrooms, sliced
- 4 chicken breasts, deboned, skinned and thinly sliced
- 2 tablespoons flour
- 1 cup milk
- 1 cup cream
- ½ cup grated Gruyere cheese
- 1 teaspoon finely chopped fresh rosemary
- ½ cup roughly chopped Italian parsley
- salt to taste
- freshly ground black pepper
- 2 cups cooked spinach, finely chopped
- 1 roll shop-bought puff pastry, defrosted
- 1 egg, beaten

Heat the butter in a saucepan, add the onion and cook for 5 minutes, stirring. Now add the garlic, mushrooms and chicken, and cook, stirring for 8 minutes.

Stir in the flour to coat the ingredients and then pour in the milk and cream – slowly! Cook till saucy, then stir in the cheese and herbs. Season with salt and pepper, and when the cheese has melted, remove from the stove and cool.

Working on a cool surface, with cool hands, roll the pastry out. Place the spinach on half of the pastry first, then top with the cooled chicken filling. Fold the remaining pastry over the filling, paint a bit of milk or water around the edges and press down to seal.

Place the pie on a baking sheet, and make a few slashes on the top of the pie so that the steam can escape. Brush the pastry with beaten egg and chill for 30 minutes.

Preheat the oven to 220 °C and bake the pie till it is golden brown and cooked through.

Serve hot with a delicious green salad.

SERVES 4–6

TIP: It might be easier to work directly on your baking tray to avoid accidents when transferring the finished pie.

I love a salad at any time of day or night, and I especially enjoy one that has juicy chicken breasts as an ingredient. Here is a quick and easy way to steam breasts to succulence! You can also give it a Chinese twist by adding ginger, soy sauce, chillies or sesame oil, and serve on rice.

Plate-steamed zesty chicken

- 2 butterflied chicken breast fillets
- 1 clove garlic, chopped
- 2 teaspoons olive oil
- salt
- freshly ground black pepper
- 1 tablespoon chopped coriander
- 1 spring onion with tops, chopped
- butter, for dotting
- zest of 1 lime
- juice of 1 lime

Lay the breasts onto a heat-proof dinner plate, rub with chopped garlic and olive oil, and season with salt and pepper. Top with coriander and spring onion, and dot with butter.

Bring a pot of water, large enough to hold the dinner plate on top, to the boil. Place the plate onto the pot and cover with another plate the same size.

Cook till the chicken is just done; remove from the heat. Keep covered for a few more minutes before serving, and then sprinkle with the lime zest and juice and serve!

SERVES 2

TIP: You can also cook fish or prawns this way.

Hot chicken livers and cumin-scented potatoes

SEASONED FLOUR
- 1 cup flour
- celery salt
- garlic salt
- freshly ground black pepper
- 1 teaspoon fresh thyme, finely chopped
- 1 teaspoon smoked paprika

CHICKEN LIVERS
- 2 large potatoes, peeled
- 100 g unsalted butter, plus a little extra
- 2 large onions, peeled and thinly sliced
- 1 teaspoon cumin seeds, toasted and bashed
- salt, to taste
- 400 g plump chicken livers, well cleaned
- 4 cloves garlic, crushed
- 1 tablespoon roughly chopped fresh coriander
- ½ cup torn fresh basil leaves
- 1 teaspoon fresh lemon zest
- juice of 1 lemon
- 1 tablespoon roughly chopped fresh Italian parsley

I love these livers to be slightly pink inside – it keeps them succulent – and then I just mop the lot up with crusty bread and some freshly chopped chilli.

Mix all the ingredients for the seasoned flour together well. Parboil the potatoes; cube them and set aside.

Heat half the butter in a non-stick frying pan; when it begins to foam add the onions and cook them gently until they are really golden and cooked down.

Remove the onions from the pan. Add half the remaining butter with the cumin seeds and cubed potatoes, season with a little salt and cook till golden without burning them. Remove from the pan and set aside. Don't wash the pan!

Toss the livers in the seasoned flour, shaking off any excess. Heat the remaining butter in the same pan, add the livers with the garlic and cook till just done, turning the entire time. Stir in the coriander and basil, and set aside.

In the same pan add the lemon zest and a little of the remaining butter; heat gently. Return the livers to the pan and toss in the lemon juice. Add the cumin potatoes and chopped parsley, and gently mix together.

Serve and mop the lot up with some really crusty bread.

SERVES 4 – 6

TIP: You can add more basil or coriander if you wish. I do; they are my favourite herbs.

> "As for those grapefruit and buttermilk diets, I'll take roast chicken and dumplings."
>
> *Hattie McDaniel*

My veri-peri chicken

You can use chicken pieces, wings and legs, or spatchcocked chickens for this. When I make up a batch of this sauce I normally make four times the amount and freeze it in zip lock bags.

- 2 big fat hens

PERI-PERI MARINADE

- 4 large red chillies, seeds removed
- 8 cloves garlic
- 1 cup fresh rosemary needles
- 3 tablespoons finely chopped fresh ginger
- 2 teaspoons ground ginger
- zest of 1 lemon
- 1 cup water
- juice of 2 lemons
- 2 large red peppers, roughly chopped
- freshly ground black pepper
- ½ cup olive oil
- 2 tablespoons toasted cumin seeds, roughly ground

Spatchcock the chickens and lay them skin-side down in a flat shallow oven-proof dish.

Blitz all the peri-peri ingredients together in your food processor, spoon into a small saucepan and cook over a low heat for 5 minutes.

Pour the sauce over the chickens, covering them completely, and marinate for 2 hours or overnight.

Preheat the oven to 190 °C. Remove the chickens from the fridge 20 minutes before cooking and season with salt and pepper. Roast for 20 minutes at 190 °C, then turn the oven down to 175 °C and roast for a further 30 minutes or until cooked through.

Serve with lemony potato wedges and a monster mixed salad!

SERVES 6–8

My spicy, chunky chicken kebabs

- 1.5 kg chicken breast fillets, skinned and deboned
- 1 level teaspoon ground ginger
- 4 cloves garlic, crushed
- 1 level teaspoon paprika
- 1 heaped teaspoon cumin seeds, toasted and roughly bashed
- ½ teaspoon ground cinnamon
- salt
- freshly ground black pepper
- runny honey, for brushing

Cut the chicken into chunks and place in a glass bowl. Add all the ingredients, except the salt, pepper and honey, and toss the chicken well so that the chunks are well coated with the spices. Marinate for 30 minutes.

Thread the chicken onto wooden skewers and season with salt and pepper. Grill the chicken skewers under a hot grill till done. Brush with honey just before serving, and seal on the heat for a few seconds.

Serve with sultana couscous, and red onions and minted yoghurt, or lemon sautéed potatoes and a large green salad.

SERVES 6

TIP: Soak your wooden skewers in water for about 20 minutes before you thread on the chicken – then the wood won't burn when you grill your kebabs.

If you add any type of acid to your marinade (like lemon juice, wine or vinegar) for chicken breasts, do not leave them soaking for longer than an hour; the flesh breaks down and becomes mealy!

Ginger, orange and duck salad

I can't say who is more in love with the other, but what I do know is that the combination of duck and orange is a match made in heaven. The wonderful, fragrant, juicy orange and the richness of the duck flesh and the saltiness of the soy with runny honey do it for me! I just love ginger – this versatile spice is so lively and it really gives any dish a bit of zing.

THE DUCK
- 3 plump duck breasts, skin scored
- salt
- freshly ground black pepper
- 1 tablespoon toasted cumin seeds, roughly ground
- 1 red onion, peeled and thinly sliced
- 4 large oranges, peeled and sliced

DRESSING IT
- 2 teaspoons olive oil
- ½ teaspoon cumin seeds
- 5 cm fresh ginger, peeled and cut into very thin strips
- peel of 2 oranges, cut into very thin strips, no pith please
- 2 tablespoons honey
- 2 cloves garlic, crushed
- 1 tablespoon soy sauce
- 1 teaspoon sesame oil
- 1 tablespoon chopped fresh coriander
- 1 tablespoon chopped fresh mint

SERVES 4

Season the duck skin with salt and pepper. Turn over and rub the ground cumin into the flesh; season with salt.

Heat a frying pan and place the duck breasts skin-side down into the pan and slowly cook them without turning till the skin is crisp and the fat is cooked out. This will take about 10 minutes; don't burn the skin! Drain the fat from the pan and keep it aside.

Place the pan back on the heat and turn the breasts onto the flesh-side and seal them – about 2 to 3 minutes. When they have a nice colour, remove them from the pan and let them rest on a plate till you need them.

To make the dressing, heat the olive oil in a small saucepan and add the cumin seeds, ginger and orange peel. Cook for 1 minute and then add the honey. When it starts to foam add the garlic and soy sauce, and cook for 1 minute. Taste the dressing and if you would like a little more soy sauce add it now.

Remove from the heat and stir in the sesame oil and herbs. Be sure to dress the salad while the dressing is still warm.

Slice the duck breasts thinly. Layer the onion and oranges on a platter and tuck in the duck slices, dress and enjoy.

TIP: A few sliced red chillies give this salad a kick!

They say: In the Melanesian Islands ginger is used to attract the opposite sex. They chew ginger in the Philippines to ward off evil spirits.

Butter chicken the way I like it

Jeff Wittels, now you have the recipe; send Myrna to that stove and let her please your taste buds!

- 3 tablespoons ghee or vegetable oil
- 6 chicken breasts, cut into bite-sized pieces and seasoned
- 1 tablespoon mustard seeds
- 1 large onion, finely chopped
- 1 tablespoon finely chopped fresh ginger
- 1 tablespoon garlic, crushed
- ½ teaspoon garam masala
- 1 teaspoon ground cumin
- 1 teaspoon ground coriander
- ½ teaspoon chilli powder
- pinch of sugar
- salt and pepper
- 3 cardamom pods, toasted and seeds ground
- 400 g large juicy tomatoes, peeled and grated
- 2 tablespoons tomato paste
- ½ cup chicken stock
- 1 cup fresh cream
- 100 g cold butter, cut into small pieces

TO GARNISH
- fresh coriander
- 4 tablespoons cashew nuts, lightly toasted and chopped

Heat 2 tablespoons of ghee or oil in a saucepan, and gently sauté the chicken pieces in batches till half cooked. Remove with a slotted spoon and set aside till later.

Add the remaining ghee to the saucepan and heat, now add the mustard seeds and fry for a few minutes so that they pop. Add the onion, ginger and garlic and cook for a few minutes till fragrant. Stir in the garam masala, cumin, coriander and chilli powder – do not let the spices burn! Add a little more ghee and cook for a few minutes.

Now add the sugar, salt, pepper, cardamom, tomatoes, tomato paste and chicken stock. Bring to the boil and cook till the sauce has become fragrant.

Pour the sauce into a food processor and blend till smooth. Return to the saucepan and add the cream. Bring the sauce to a simmer, adjust the seasoning, and return the chicken to the pot. Warm through.

Just before you are ready to serve, stir in the chopped butter a few pieces at a time. Spoon the butter chicken into a bowl, and garnish with coriander and chopped cashew nuts.

Serve with steaming hot basmati rice.

SERVES 4

We all know that chefs by nature hate strangers coming into their territory, but I have been so fortunate and have been welcomed into many wonderful kitchens around the world. I think it is so generous of chefs to allow someone else who is passionate about food into their kitchens – because that's how you get to understand how flavours work.

My honey ginger orange duck

It took me years before I could place a moist, delicious morsel of duck into my mouth without the name Jemima popping into my head – I'm talking Jemima Puddle Duck. I had a duck called Daffy when I was young; if I knew then what I know now!

THE DUCK
- 1 whole, voluptuous duck
- 2 star anise
- ½ cup soy sauce
- 2 slices fresh ginger

THE RUB
- 1 tablespoon fennel seeds
- 1 tablespoon cumin seeds
- 1 tablespoon coriander seeds
- 2 teaspoons Sichuan peppercorns

THE MARINADE
- 4 tablespoons chopped fresh ginger
- zest of 2 oranges
- 3 whole star anise
- ¾ cup honey
- 4 cloves garlic, crushed
- ½ cup soy sauce
- 1 cup ruby port
- juice of 2 oranges
- 10 ml sesame oil
- pinch of ground cinnamon

SOY FRIED NOODLES
- 1 tablespoon sunflower oil
- 1 teaspoon sesame oil
- 2 fat cloves garlic, crushed
- 100 g mange tout, thinly sliced
- 1 carrot, cut into thin matchsticks
- 3 blocks pre-soaked Chinese egg noodles
- 4 tablespoons soy sauce
- small handful fresh coriander, roughly chopped

Place the duck in a pot large enough to hold it. Add the star anise, soy and ginger; now cover the duck with water (this is to get a measurement of how much water you need). Remove the duck from the pot and heat the liquid. Return the duck to the pot and simmer for 20 minutes.

Remove the duck from the pot, place on a tray and prick the skin all over. Place the duck in front of a fan and let the skin dry.

In the meantime mix the rub. Dry-toast the seeds with the Sichuan pepper and grind to a rough texture.

Oil the duck gently, and rub the spice mix onto the breasts, the legs and the thighs; turn it over and give the back a rub now. Let it rest while you prepare the marinade.

Mix all the marinade ingredients together, except the sesame oil and the cinnamon, and place them in a saucepan. Cook down gently and when the marinade is nice and syrupy, stir in the sesame oil and cinnamon.

Place the duck onto a hot baking tray and put into the oven at 190 °C and cook for 10 minutes. Now paint the duck all over with the marinade and return to the oven. Repeat the painting process about 3 times, cooking for 30 minutes.

Turn the oven down to 160 °C and paint that duck again. Cook for a further 20 minutes, then wiggle the legs and if they feel loose, remove the duck from the oven and let it rest for about 10 minutes before serving.

While the duck is resting, prepare the noodles. Heat the oils in a large frying pan, and add the garlic, mange tout and carrot sticks. Cook stirring for 2 minutes, then add the pre-soaked noodles and soy sauce; heat through and stir in the coriander.

Serve the duck on a bed of soy fried noodles and drizzle with any left-over marinade – make sure that it's warm now!

SERVES 4

TIP: If you can't find Sichuan peppercorns, use 1 teaspoon bashed white peppercorns instead.

CHAPTER TEN

Magnificent,
Meaty Mains

Sunday lunches were very special when I was a child;
they were tasty, happy moments spent in the kitchen
with my mother.

That woman had worked all week, yet she would start her
day at the normal 5 am, in the kitchen preparing a feast that
usually included two meats and more vegetables than I could
count. I always wondered where she got the energy.

We would wake up to wonderful fragrances wafting
down the passage; the familiar aroma of huge legs of mutton,
scented with herbs, roasting in the oven. It took a bit longer
to cook than lamb, so she started early, but she loved its
intense flavour, especially with lots of garlic and rosemary.
My sister Beverley and I would fight over the sticky, salty
bones once the leg was carved; she always won!

My mother was also very good at making braised steak.
She used to cut thick slabs of beef, peel mounds of onions
and garlic and slice them thickly, then add lots of chunky,
sweet carrots that were plucked fresh from the earth before
they hit the pot. Just before dinner she would send me out to
pick a bunch of fresh thyme to infuse the meat with flavour,
and then she would serve it all up with mounds of mashed
potatoes whipped up with masses of salty butter.

What a delicious childhood I had!

"Hunger finds
no fault with
the cook."
Unknown

"What do you mean you don't eat no meat? ... That's okay, I'll make lamb."
Aunt Voula in 'My Big Fat Greek Wedding'

Herbed rack of lamb

I love the way my home smells while the lamb roasts!

- 2 tablespoons fresh rosemary needles
- 2 tablespoons toasted cumin seeds, ground
- 2 tablespoons toasted coriander seeds, ground
- 2 tablespoons toasted caraway seeds or fennel seeds, ground
- 1 tablespoon lemon zest
- 4 cloves garlic, crushed
- 2 tablespoons olive oil
- 1 cup fresh breadcrumbs
- 2 racks of lamb, with 8 cutlets each
- salt
- freshly ground black pepper
- 2 tablespoons ready-made English mustard

Preheat the oven to 200 °C. Mix together the rosemary, cumin, coriander, caraway, lemon zest, garlic, olive oil and breadcrumbs.

Season the lamb racks well with salt and pepper. Heat a little olive oil in a frying pan and brown the lamb all over. Place on a roasting tray and spread each rack with mustard. Divide the herb crumbs and press them onto the racks. Roast for about 45 to 50 minutes, or till done the way you like them.

Rest before carving so that all the delicious juices go back into the meat! Serve with crisp and sticky lemony roasted potatoes, roasted butternut salad and some buttery green beans.

SERVES 4

166

Succulent lamb kebabs

- 1.5 kg deboned leg of lamb, cut into bite-sized cubes
- 3 cloves garlic, crushed
- ¼ teaspoon ground cloves
- 1 teaspoon white pepper
- ½ teaspoon ground cinnamon
- 1 teaspoon ground cumin
- 1 ⅓ teaspoons ground allspice
- zest of 1 ripe lemon
- juice of 1 lemon
- 3 tablespoons olive oil
- 1 tablespoon finely chopped rosemary needles

Who can resist a juicy, tender slice of free-range lamb!

Place the lamb cubes in a glass bowl and add the remaining ingredients. Rub the spices into the lamb and marinate for a couple of hours in the fridge.

Soak as many wooden skewers as you need in warm water for about 20 minutes. Thread the lamb onto the skewers and grill or barbeque the kebabs till they are done the way you like them.

Serve with a yoghurt and mint drizzle, a big couscous and roasted vegetable salad, and some crunchy green leaves. They also work well with a pile of buttery pine nut and saffron rice.

SERVES 4 – 6

Breyani for Mommy Ruby

- 1.5 kg leg of lamb

FOR THE MARINADE
- 120 g grated onions
- 30 g grated fresh ginger
- 1 tablespoon chilli powder
- 1 teaspoon ground cinnamon
- ⅔ teaspoon ground cardamom
- 1 teaspoon ground coriander powder
- ½ teaspoon caraway seeds
- ½ teaspoon ground nutmeg
- ½ teaspoon ground mace
- ¾ cup Greek yoghurt

FOR THE RICE
- 500 g basmati rice, well washed
- 4 tablespoons ghee
- 3 cups water
- ½ cup milk
- 4 potatoes, peeled and cubed
- 5 saffron strands, or egg yellow colouring

For my sweet Durban mother, Ruby Naidu; you will always be remembered for your energy and love, breyani and crab curry!

Cube the lamb and place in a large, flat dish. Mix all the marinade ingredients together and pour over the lamb. Mix well and allow to soak for 3 to 4 hours.

Place the rice in a saucepan with half the ghee, the water and milk. Cook until half-done then remove from the stove. Heat the remaining ghee in a frying pan and brown the potatoes. Set aside.

Place the meat with the marinade in a large oven-proof dish, cover with the potatoes, followed by the rice. Mix the saffron with 2 tablespoons of water and pour over the rice. Cover tightly and bake in the oven at 170 °C for 2 hours.

Serve with sambals and raita.

SERVE 4 – 6

This is such a delicious lunch in a wrap. So dig in on the double, dears!

Lamb wraps

THE LAMB

- 1 kg deboned leg of lamb, cut into 6 slices
- olive oil
- salt
- freshly ground black pepper
- 1 tablespoon cumin seeds
- 6 tortilla wraps

THE SALAD

- 1 red onion, thinly sliced
- 3 spring onions with tops, sliced
- 2 cloves garlic, crushed
- 1 medium English cucumber, cubed
- zest of 1 ripe lemon
- 1 green chilli, chopped
- ½ cup freshly chopped mint
- ½ cup freshly chopped coriander
- ½ cup freshly chopped flat leaf parsley
- salt
- freshly ground black pepper
- 1 cup Greek yoghurt

Rub the lamb slices with olive oil, season with salt and freshly ground black pepper, and press into the cumin seeds.

Heat a non-stick frying pan and add a little olive oil, sear the lamb slices on both sides, and cook till slightly pink. Rest the meat and slice each of the 6 pieces thinly when the salad is ready.

Mix all the salad ingredients together and place onto a platter. Top with sliced lamb.

Warm the wraps in a dry pan, place them onto a wooden board and let everyone fill their own with lamb salad.

SERVES 6

Lamb as the Sunday roast has always been my preference; it is so easy to cook, it is succulent and it absorbs flavours so readily from other ingredients. I love lamb that has roasted just till it is slightly pink. Or doing it Greek-style, long and slow, but with all the juices still left to flow. I love the delicious smells of fresh rosemary, lemon and garlic wafting enticingly through the house.

Roasted stuffed lamb in a rosemary pastry jacket

THE LAMB
- 1.5 kg – 2 kg deboned leg of lamb
- olive oil
- salt
- freshly ground black pepper

THE STUFFING
- 50 g fresh breadcrumbs made from day-old bread
- ¼ cup chopped fresh rosemary
- 4 anchovies, finely chopped
- 6 cloves garlic, chopped
- zest of 2 lemons
- juice of 1 lemon
- 2 spring onions, finely chopped
- ½ cup sultanas, finely chopped
- ½ cup dates, finely chopped
- freshly ground black pepper
- 1 teaspoon cumin seeds, roasted and roughly bashed
- 1 egg yolk, beaten

THE PASTRY JACKET
- 1 roll shop-bought puff pastry
- 2 tablespoons soft butter
- 2 tablespoons apricot jam
- salt
- freshly ground black pepper
- ¼ cup fresh rosemary needles
- 2 cloves garlic, crushed
- zest of 1 fresh lemon
- 1 egg, beaten

Preheat the oven to 200 °C. Open up the leg of lamb and oil lightly all over; season well with salt and pepper.

Mix together the ingredients for the stuffing and spread over the lamb. Tuck in the sides and roll the lamb up. Tie it off with string in about six places.

Heat a little oil in a large frying pan and seal the lamb on all sides, giving it some nice colour.

Place the lamb in the oven and roast for 40 minutes. Remove from the oven, set aside to cool, and then remove the string.

You could prepare up to this point the day before and then finish it off on the day. Keep the lamb in the fridge, but bring it to room temperature before covering with the pastry.

Roll the pastry out to fit the lamb with enough space to fold over and seal. Spread the butter over the pastry, then spread the apricot jam, season over that with salt and pepper, and lastly sprinkle with the rosemary needles, garlic and lemon zest.

Preheat the oven to 200 °C. Place the lamb in the centre of the pastry and cover, sealing in the edges. Place the parcel seal-side down on a roasting tray and give the pastry an egg wash with beaten egg. Cut a few air holes in the top of the pastry for the steam to escape.

Bake in the hot oven till the pastry is puffed up and golden; about 25 minutes. Cover with foil if it starts browning too fast.

Remove from the oven and rest before carving. Serve with roast potatoes and a selection of crunchy green vegetables and roasted butternut.

SERVES 4 – 6

Braised lamb with butter beans

This mouth never gets homesick while I am travelling, until I land on home ground. Then what I want is a succulent lamb stew.

This stew is utter comfort for me and I love to serve it with either polenta or steamed nutty brown rice. I love the texture of a butter bean; it is creamy and full of flavour. You can also make this a meatless meal if you have a vegetarian around for dinner – just stew the beans without the meat.

- 3 tablespoons olive oil
- 1.5 kg lamb neck pieces
- flour for dusting
- salt
- freshly ground black pepper
- 2 large onions, finely chopped
- 6 cloves garlic, crushed
- ½ teaspoon ground cinnamon
- 1 teaspoon ground cumin
- 3 ripe tomatoes, chopped
- 3 tablespoons tomato purée
- 2 sticks celery, chopped
- 1 carrot, chopped
- 1 teaspoon freshly chopped rosemary needles
- 1 ½ cups chicken stock
- 3 cups cooked butter beans
- fresh coriander

Place the oil in a saucepan large enough to hold the lamb and beans. Dust the lamb with flour, and season with salt and pepper. Brown in batches and set aside. If you need to add a little more oil to the pot, do so. Remove the meat from the pot and set aside.

Add the onions to the pot and brown gently, then add the garlic, cinnamon and cumin. Cook, stirring for 2 minutes. Add the tomatoes, tomato purée, celery, carrot and rosemary and give it a good stir.

Return the meat to the pot. Pour over the stock and simmer till just before the meat becomes tender. Adjust the seasoning, add the butter beans and simmer gently for 30 minutes.

Check for textures; everything should be cooked through but not mushy. Chop the coriander and scatter over the top. Dinner is ready!

SERVES 4 – 6

TIP: This can be made the day before; reheat gently in the oven at 180° C for about 15 minutes, and serve.

Okay boys, this dish is simple and easy enough to prepare. This gives us girls the night off – time to take a nice deep bubble bath and hello, no headache!

Slow, lazy man lamb

THE VEGETABLES
- 6 celery stalks, roughly chopped
- 4 peeled carrots, roughly chopped
- 1 large head of garlic
- 2 onions, peeled and thickly sliced
- 4 large potatoes, washed and cut into thick rounds
- 1 teaspoon dried oregano
- 1 tablespoon olive oil
- salt and pepper

THE LAMB
- 2 kg free-range lamb, (nice-sized leg or shoulder)
- 1 tablespoon olive oil
- salt and pepper
- large stem fresh rosemary
- 1 cup chicken or vegetable stock
- juice of 1 lemon

Preheat the oven to 160 °C. Toss all the vegetable ingredients together and place them at the bottom of a large roasting pan.

Oil the lamb and season with salt and pepper. Brown gently in a frying pan and remove. Place the rosemary stem onto the vegetables, top with the lamb, pour in the stock and lemon juice, and seal with foil. Just forget about it for 2 ½ hours.

Check for tenderness. (Now, how do you explain that to a man!) You will know that the meat is ready when it falls away from the bone.

Serve with a mound of buttery, garlicky polenta.

SERVES 4

Pork schnitzel

When cooking pork, cook till you just take away the pink and it will be all juicy and succulent.

THE CRUMBS
- 2 cups fresh breadcrumbs
- ¼ teaspoon ground cloves
- 1 teaspoon paprika
- salt and pepper
- 2 tablespoons sesame seeds
- oil for frying

THE PORK
- 4 x 200 g pork schnitzels, flattened
- 4 tablespoons flour
- 2 eggs, beaten

Mix the breadcrumbs with the cloves, paprika, salt, pepper and sesame seeds.

Season the pork schnitzels, dust with flour, dip into the beaten egg and then coat them with the seasoned breadcrumbs. Rest in the fridge till the breadcrumbs set.

Heat the oil in a large non-stick frying pan and fry the schnitzels till golden and crisp; drain on paper towels.

Serve with green onion mash and apple-braised red cabbage – pure comfort!

SERVES 4

Tropical pork chops

Rich and succulent pork chops, beautiful and pale pink, begging to be taken home and tossed in a pan. Team up with pineapple – a match made in heaven – add some fresh ginger and you have a really great chop.

THE CHOPS
- 4 thick lean pork loin chops
- salt
- freshly ground black pepper
- olive oil

TOP WITH
- 4 teaspoons softened butter
- ¼ teaspoon ground cloves
- 2 cloves garlic, crushed
- 1 teaspoon grated fresh ginger
- 4 tablespoons very finely chopped fresh pineapple
- 1 heaped tablespoon soft brown sugar
- pinch of salt

Season the pork chops with salt and pepper. Heat a little olive oil in a frying pan and seal the chops; do not cook through, just long enough in the pan to give them a little colour. Remove from the pan and place in a roasting pan.

Mix the topping ingredients together and spread over the chops. Bake at 180 °C till the topping is all sticky and gooey; about 8 to 10 minutes.

Serve with an oven-baked potato and a green salad.

SERVES 4

TRY THIS: Once you have tossed your chops in the pan, top with tomato, a fresh sage leaf and mozzarella wrapped in bacon. Bake them in the oven at 180 °C just till the mozzarella melts and the bacon is cooked, and serve them on a pile of creamy deep-fried caper polenta with rich tomato sauce.

> "One of the very nicest things about life is the way we must regularly stop whatever it is we are doing and devote our attention to eating."
> *Luciano Pavarotti*

Roasted pork neck with tomato sauce

When you buy the pork neck, ask your butcher to put it into a net for you. Serve on a pile of Parmesan polenta or butter bean mash, accompanied by a mound of buttery, steamed baby beans and a fresh salad dressed with vinaigrette.

THE PORK
- 1 rolled deboned pork neck, about 1.5 kg
- olive oil
- salt
- freshly ground black pepper
- 1 tablespoon finely chopped fresh rosemary
- capers, for garnishing
- chopped fresh parsley, for garnishing

THE TOMATO SAUCE
- olive oil for frying
- 1 large onion, finely chopped
- 2 cloves garlic, chopped
- 1 chilli (optional)
- 2 sticks celery, finely chopped
- 2 x 400 g canned tomatoes with their juice
- ½ glass red wine
- pinch of sugar
- 2 teaspoons fresh thyme leaves
- 2 sage leaves, thinly sliced
- small pinch of cinnamon
- 1 small clove garlic, crushed
- some chopped celery leaves

Preheat the oven to 180 °C. Rub the pork with olive oil and season well with salt and pepper; then rub the chopped rosemary into the pork.

Heat some olive oil in a large frying pan and gently brown the meat on all sides. Place the meat on an oven tray and roast for about 1 ½ hours till just cooked.

In the meantime, make the tomato sauce. Heat a little olive oil in a saucepan and gently fry the onion, garlic, chilli and celery till they are translucent. Add the tomatoes and cook gently till the juice has cooked right down.

Add the red wine and simmer for 5 minutes. Add a pinch of sugar to balance the dish, and toss in the fresh thyme. Cook for a further 5 minutes.

Taste the sauce and adjust the seasoning. Add the sage, stir in the cinnamon and garlic, and simmer for 10 minutes more. Stir in some chopped celery leaves, not too much now, and serve the sauce with the roast pork.

The pork can be sliced thickly and left to rest in the sauce until ready to serve. Don't throw the pan juices away; add them to the sauce. Garnish with capers and lots of freshly chopped Italian parsley.

SERVES 4 – 6

TIP: I'm watching some of you poking your meat with a knife. Please don't do this because it makes the juices run out of the meat and it will dry out and be tough.

All sticky and licky, this is my version of Chinese pork ribs. It is one of the dishes that the people on my cooking trips to China just couldn't get enough of! You could do the same with tender beef or lamb ribs, if you like.

Sticky pork ribs

- 2 kg pork ribs, cut into portions

FOR THE MARINADE
- ½ cup tomato sauce
- 6 tablespoons dry sherry
- 2 teaspoons Chinese five-spice powder
- 1 cup hoisin sauce
- 1 tablespoon dark soy sauce
- 1 tablespoon grated fresh ginger
- 4 cloves garlic, crushed
- 1 tablespoon runny honey
- zest of 1 orange
- 1 red chilli

Preheat the oven to 200 °C. Give all the marinade ingredients a whizz in a food processor. Place the ribs in a container with a tight-fitting lid, and pour the marinade over. Make sure that you coat the ribs well in the marinade, and place them in the fridge overnight, so that the ingredients can get to know each other.

Place a wire rack over a roasting pan containing 500 ml of water. Pack the ribs onto the rack and bake for 25 minutes on one side, then turn the ribs and cook the other side for about 20 minutes.

Check the ribs for tenderness and if they seem to be ready, remove from the oven and rest for a few minutes before eating them.

If they seem a little tough, let them continue to cook till they are tender and the bone moves with ease when pulled. Keep an eye on them so that they do not burn; you don't want them to taste all bitter now, just sticky and sweet.

Serve with a green salad and a baked potato, or with a bowl of noodles and vegetables. Don't forget a finger bowl for each person!

SERVES 6

TIP: Baste the ribs while they are cooking so that the sweet marinade sticks to the flesh.

"If you want dinner,
don't offend the cook."
Chinese proverb

Bacon-wrapped beef fillet stuffed with cranberries and Turkish apricots

THE FILLING

- 300 g chicken breast, chopped
- 2 tablespoons chopped thyme
- 2 tablespoons chopped rosemary
- 1 tablespoon minced garlic
- 2 tablespoons grated fresh ginger
- 4 spring onions with tops, thinly sliced
- 12 prunes, chopped
- 150 g chopped dried Turkish apricots
- 150 g roughly chopped dried cranberries
- salt and pepper

THE BEEF

- 1 x 1.5 kg beef fillet
- 24 slices streaky bacon

A delicious combination with beef; the salty, smoky bacon and sundried fruit is a match made in heaven!

Mix all the filling ingredients together in a bowl, and season with salt and pepper.

Open the fillet by starting to slice from the centre lengthwise, and work your way out till it is at least three times wider.

Preheat the oven to 180 °C. Stuff the fillet with the filling and roll it up; season well with salt and pepper.

Lay the bacon out onto a flat surface, one piece to the left and one to the right, overlapping a little bit in the centre all the way down the length of the fillet.

Place the stuffed fillet onto the bacon and, starting from the top, gently close the fillet by folding alternate strips of bacon over it, almost making a plait. Pin the top of the bacon with toothpicks should you have difficulty in keeping it all together.

Gently lift the wrapped fillet into a preheated pan and cook the fillet seal-side down to close it. Transfer it onto your oven tray and roast at 180 °C for 30 to 35 minutes. Remove from the oven and rest the meat for 10 minutes before carving.

Serve hot or cold with roast potatoes and seasonal veggies or salads.

SERVES 6

Whole honey soy fillet topped with toasted sesame seeds

- 1 whole beef fillet (minimum 2 kg)
- 1 tablespoon olive oil
- 3 cloves garlic, crushed
- salt
- white pepper
- 2 tablespoons sesame seeds, toasted, for garnishing

HONEY AND SOY BASTE
- 2 tablespoons oil
- 2 tablespoons chopped fresh ginger
- 2 cloves garlic, crushed
- 2 tablespoons full cream sherry
- grated zest and juice of 1 orange
- 1 tablespoon brown sugar
- 2 tablespoons runny honey
- 5 tablespoons soy sauce
- 1 tablespoon oyster sauce
- 1 teaspoon sesame oil
- 3 spring onions, thinly sliced
- small handful coriander, chopped
- small handful fresh mint, chopped

Whenever I feast on a whole fillet with my friends and family, I think of Whitey Basson who has a passion for Good Meat. This recipe is for you Mr B!

Preheat the oven to 200 °C. Rub the fillet all over with the oil and then rub with the crushed garlic; season well with salt and pepper. Heat a large non-stick frying pan and sear the fillet on all sides so it has an even colour. Remove the fillet from the pan and place onto a baking sheet.

Make the honey and soy baste next. Heat the oil in a saucepan and gently cook the ginger for a minute, stirring so it does not burn. Add the garlic and cook for 20 seconds and then add all the remaining ingredients and boil rapidly for 5 minutes. Turn down the heat and simmer for a further 5 minutes.

Brush the fillet all over with the honey soy glaze and place into the preheated oven. After the fillet has been in the oven for 8 minutes, brush again with the basting sauce, and cook to the way you like it.

Remove from the oven, sprinkle the toasted sesame seeds onto the meat and let the fillet rest for a few minutes.

Slice at the table, and give it a drizzle of basting sauce just before serving.

Serve with stir-fried vegetable noodles. Delicious!

SERVES 6 – 8

On my last trip to Bangkok I had the most amazing beef and mushroom salad. It was one of the rare times that I ate at my hotel, and this is my spin on it.

Warm beef and mushroom salad

THE BEEF
- 1 tablespoon olive oil
- 500 g fillet or sirloin steak
- salt and white pepper
- 1 teaspoon ground cumin
- 120 g cos lettuce

THE MUSHROOMS
- 3 tablespoons olive oil
- 150 g porcini mushrooms, sliced
- 100 g enoki, or mixed fresh mushrooms
- 1 red chilli, sliced (optional)
- 3 cloves garlic, chopped
- 1 red pepper, very thinly sliced
- 2 tablespoons dark soy sauce
- 3 spring onions with tops, sliced
- ½ cup chopped Italian parsley
- 2 tablespoons toasted sesame seeds

THE DRESSING
- 2 tablespoons sunflower oil
- juice of 1 lime
- 1 teaspoon fish sauce
- 1 teaspoon sesame oil
- 2 spring onions with tops, chopped
- 1 tablespoon light soy sauce
- 1 teaspoon brown sugar
- 1 teaspoon grated fresh ginger
- 2 tablespoons chopped fresh coriander

Prepare the beef first. Oil the beef and season with salt, pepper and cumin. Heat a non-stick frying pan and sear the beef on all sides, continue cooking to your desired doneness (although I am going to recommend you cook it medium-rare). Let the beef cool and rest for an hour before you need it.

Prepare the mushrooms next. Heat the olive oil in a frying pan and fry the mushrooms till they start to wilt. Add the chilli, garlic, red pepper and soy sauce, and cook for 2 minutes. Remove from the heat. Stir in the spring onions, parsley and half of the sesame seeds, and set aside.

When you are ready to start thinking about assembling the salad, shake all the dressing ingredients together in a jar. Slice the beef thinly and coat with the dressing. Mix the beef with the mushrooms.

Arrange the lettuce on a large platter, pile the mushrooms and beef onto that, and serve garnished with the remaining sesame seeds and some sliced spring onions.

SERVES 4 – 6

CHAPTER ELEVEN

My *Meatless* Oneday

Thinking back to my childhood spent in gardens with parents and grandparents who were passionate about growing, cooking and eating their own home-grown produce, it's not at all surprising that I have made food my life. I think that this thing our whole family has for gardening and edible plants stems from that.

I can't remember anywhere we lived where we couldn't get something fresh to eat from right outside our own back door; vegetables, fruit, herbs. My father wouldn't allow us to buy anything from the market if we grew it ourselves. If it didn't grow in our garden, we could buy it – which left only mushrooms really.

The biggest garden we had was when we lived in a pink cottage in Lily Vale Road in Pinetown. Inside the gate was a rose bush with tiny, creamy pink roses on it and their perfume would hit you right away. I remember sitting on the back steps with my dad eating a simple tomato sandwich, and plucking fat, sweet-smelling, sun-ripened grapes straight off the vine.

"Vegetables are a must on a diet. I suggest carrot cake, zucchini bread, and pumpkin pie."
Jim Davis

I really do enjoy meat, but I also love vegetarian dishes with a passion. I never feel deprived if I have a meatless meal, because there is such a huge variety of rich and delicious, well-balanced vegetarian dishes that will have you looking for more!

Barley risotto with roasted butternut for my boys

Peter and Greg just love barley. I also love this earthy grain and think we don't eat nearly enough of it!

FOR THE BARLEY

- 3 tablespoons unsalted butter
- 1 large onion, finely chopped
- 2 cloves garlic, crushed
- 2 leeks, sliced
- 1 cup pearl barley, washed and cooked till tender
- 1 cup hot chicken or vegetable stock

THINGS TO STIR IN

- 1 butternut, peeled and cubed
- 1 teaspoon brown sugar
- 1 tablespoon olive oil
- salt, to taste
- freshly ground black pepper
- 1 tablespoon fresh thyme
- 4 tablespoons mascarpone
- 100 g Parmesan cheese
- 3 tablespoons chopped flat leaf parsley
- 50 g pumpkin seeds or pine nuts, toasted

Prepare the barley first. Heat the butter gently and slowly cook down the onion, garlic and leeks, without browning them.

Stir in the barley and coat with the onions. Stir in half the hot stock, season and cook, stirring for 5 minutes. Then cover and simmer gently. When the liquid has nearly cooked away, add the remaining stock and cook for a further 7 minutes. The barley should be tender and not too dry; add more stock if needed.

Preheat the oven to 200 °C. Place the butternut onto a roasting tray. Sprinkle with sugar, toss in the oil, season with salt and pepper, and scatter with the thyme. Roast till golden and fork tender. Remove the butternut from the oven and stir it into the risotto with the mascarpone, Parmesan and parsley.

Serve the risotto in individual bowls, scattered with toasted pumpkin seeds.

SERVES 4

I eat this as a main course lunch with lots of chewy, crusty ciabatta and extra olive oil. This recipe is for sweet Edward Davids who supplies me with so many beautiful fresh courgettes because he does not know what to do with them all!

Roast aubergine and courgette salad

ROASTED VEGETABLES
- 4 large, long, heavy aubergines
- salt
- olive oil
- 6 courgettes, sliced lengthways
- ½ cup roughly chopped fresh coriander
- 3 tablespoons pine nuts, toasted

DRESSING
- ½ cup tahini
- 1 clove garlic, crushed
- ½ cup freshly squeezed lemon juice
- zest of 1 very ripe lemon
- 3 tablespoons warm water
- ½ cup Greek yoghurt
- ½ cup extra virgin olive oil
- salt, to taste
- freshly ground black pepper
- ¾ cup roughly chopped flat leaf parsley

Preheat the oven to 190 °C. Cut the aubergine lengthways into thick slices. Salt the slices and sweat them for 20 minutes.

In the meantime, oil the courgette slices, lay them on a baking sheet and grill until golden.

Your aubergine should be ready by now. Rinse the slices well, pat dry and paint with olive oil. Lay them on a baking sheet and grill until golden.

Blend all the dressing ingredients, except the parsley, until well incorporated. Stir in the parsley at the end.

Arrange the grilled vegetables onto a platter and spoon over the dressing. Scatter over the coriander and pine nuts, and drizzle with a little more olive oil.

SERVES 4

Aubergine and ricotta bake

TOMATO SAUCE

- 3 x 410 g cans chopped tomatoes, or 1 kg fresh chopped tomatoes
- ½ cup cream
- 1 clove garlic, crushed
- 1 teaspoon dried oregano
- salt
- freshly ground black pepper
- pinch of sugar

AUBERGINES

- 4 large aubergines, sliced in rounds and salted
- olive oil, for frying
- 1 tablespoon olive oil
- 6 whole spring onions, chopped
- 3 cloves garlic, finely chopped
- 1 red pepper finely chopped
- 400 g ricotta cheese
- ½ cup freshly chopped Italian parsley
- 2 tablespoons basil pesto
- 2 beaten eggs
- 1 cup cream
- salt
- freshly ground black pepper
- 1 cup grated Parmesan cheese, divided into 3

Heat all the ingredients for the tomato sauce together in a saucepan, and cook till the tomato breaks down and is nice and thick.

Drain the salted aubergine slices in a colander for 30 minutes, then wash the salt from them and dry them well. Fry the aubergines on one side, drain on paper towels and set aside till needed.

Heat 1 tablespoon of olive oil in a frying pan and add the spring onions, garlic and red pepper, and fry gently till wilted.

Mix together the ricotta, parsley, pesto, eggs and cream into the spring onion mixture. Season with salt and pepper, and mix thoroughly.

Divide the aubergines into 3 portions and the ricotta mixture in half. Cover the bottom of an oiled oven-proof dish with sliced aubergine, top with half the ricotta mix, half the tomato sauce and a third of the Parmesan cheese.

Repeat the layers – first aubergine, then ricotta mix, followed by tomato and Parmesan. Cover this with the remaining aubergine slices and dust with the rest of the Parmesan cheese.

Bake at 180 °C for 20 to 30 minutes. Serve hot or cold.

SERVES 4 – 6

There is nothing more delicious than a courgette picked straight from the plant. There are so many ways to prepare them; this is a favourite of mine. I serve the cakes with a garlic and fresh dill yoghurt sauce.

When buying courgettes for this recipe, buy small firm ones!

Courgette cakes

YOGHURT SAUCE
- 2 cloves garlic, crushed
- 1 tablespoon chopped mint
- 1 spring onion with tops, very finely chopped
- 1 tablespoon lemon juice
- 1 teaspoon lemon zest
- 2 tablespoons chopped fresh dill
- salt, to taste
- freshly ground black pepper
- 1 tablespoon extra virgin olive oil
- 1½ cups natural yoghurt

COURGETTE CAKES
- 500 g courgettes, grated
- 1 large potato, peeled
- 1 onion, peeled and very finely chopped
- 3 cloves garlic, finely chopped
- 1 tablespoon butter
- 2 tablespoons chopped flat leaf parsley
- ½ cup fresh breadcrumbs
- 2 tablespoons sesame seeds
- 1 teaspoon ground cumin
- 2 small eggs, beaten
- 1 small chilli, chopped (optional)
- 2 tablespoons cooked lentils
- salt, to taste
- freshly ground black pepper
- flour, for dusting
- oil, for shallow frying

Stir all the ingredients for the sauce together; taste, adjust the seasoning and chill for an hour.

Salt the grated courgettes lightly and leave to drain in a colander for 30 minutes. Rinse the salt off and dry well. Grate the potato; rinse and dry well. Place the courgettes in a large mixing bowl with the potato.

Cook the onion with the garlic in the butter for 2 minutes; spoon into the mixing bowl with the courgettes. Add the parsley, breadcrumbs, sesame seeds, cumin, beaten eggs, chilli and lentils, and season with salt and pepper. Mix well to combine the ingredients. Chill the mixture for 30 minutes so that the flavours can get to know each other.

Before you shape into patties, fry a little of the mixture to check the taste and consistency. Adjust the seasoning if need be, and add more breadcrumbs if the mixture is too soft. Shape the patties and dust with flour.

Heat the oil in a shallow pan and fry until crisp and golden. Drain on paper towels. Serve the cakes with the chilled yoghurt sauce.

SERVES 4

TIP: This sauce is also delicious with fried fish or calamari.

Aubergine and potato layered bake

- 3 cups homemade tomato sauce
- 3 cups cheese sauce
- ¾ cup grated Parmesan cheese
- pinch of grated nutmeg
- 2 tablespoons dry white wine
- 1 large aubergine
- salt
- 3 tablespoons olive oil
- 2 large courgettes
- 2 large peeled potatoes, lightly boiled
- salt and black pepper
- ¾ cup chopped parsley
- grated Parmesan cheese, for dusting

Make the tomato sauce according to the instructions on page 78, and set aside until required.

Make the cheese sauce next. Follow the recipe on page 80 for a basic white sauce, but add ¾ cup grated Parmesan cheese, a pinch of nutmeg and 2 tablespoons of dry white wine at the end. Set aside.

Cut the aubergine into medium slices, sprinkle with salt and leave to drain in a colander for 30 minutes. Rinse the salt off the aubergine and pat dry. Heat half the oil in a frying pan and lightly fry the aubergine slices on both sides, then remove from the pan and set aside.

Cut the courgettes lengthways into thick slices and fry them lightly in the same pan.

Cut the boiled potatoes into thick slices, add some more oil to the pan and give them a little colour; season with salt and pepper while they are cooking.

Now let's put it together. Place a third of the tomato sauce on the base of a medium-sized flat oven-proof dish. Arrange the potatoes on the bottom, sprinkle with a third of the parsley and cover with a third of the cheese sauce.

Now repeat the layering and saucing, starting with the courgettes and ending with cheese sauce. Repeat one last time with the aubergine slices.

Dust the surface with grated Parmesan and bake for 30 to 35 minutes at 180 °C till hot and bubbly. Serve with a huge, crunchy green salad.

SERVES 4

Broad beans on toast

- 2 tablespoons olive oil
- 2 cloves garlic, finely chopped
- 2 cups broad beans, shelled and lightly steamed
- zest of 1 ripe lemon
- salt and black pepper
- 2 long slices of grilled ciabatta
- shaved Parmesan cheese
- extra virgin olive oil, for drizzling
- lemon wedges (optional)

Heat the olive oil in a frying pan and add the garlic. Stir for 20 seconds and then add the beans and lemon zest. Roughly mash the beans while they are warming through, season with salt and pepper, and remove from the stove.

Place the grilled ciabatta onto a plate, divide the beans and pile them on top. Scatter over some shaved Parmesan, drizzle with extra virgin olive oil, splash over the juice from a lemon wedge or two, and tuck in.

SERVES 2

EXTRAS: Serve a fresh rocket salad on the side and if you want to make a special breakfast, top with shaved Parma ham and a soft poached egg.

I love aubergine! They are robust with a wonderful meaty texture. I always salt aubergines before cooking, not only to purge them of bitterness, but salting collapses the membranes and then they tend to absorb less oil.

Aubergine cannelloni

- 2 ½ cups homemade tomato sauce
- 3 aubergines weighing about 250 g each
- 75 ml olive oil
- 250 g ricotta cheese
- 75 g freshly grated Parmesan cheese
- ½ cup fresh cream
- 1 egg, beaten
- 1 cup cooked, chopped spinach
- ½ teaspoon ground nutmeg
- 2 cloves garlic, crushed
- 8 large basil leaves, shredded
- salt, to taste
- freshly ground black pepper
- 50 g grated mozzarella, for sprinkling
- 50 g grated Parmesan, for sprinkling

Make the tomato sauce according to the recipe on page 78.

Preheat the oven to 190 °C. Slice the aubergines lengthways into thin slices. Salt lightly and let them sweat for 30 minutes; wash and pat dry. Brush the aubergine with olive oil and fry gently on both sides. Lay the slices onto a flat surface and mix the filling.

Place the ricotta, Parmesan, cream, egg, spinach, nutmeg, garlic and basil into a mixing bowl. Season with salt and pepper, and mix well together.

Divide the filling between the sliced aubergines. Place a portion of filling onto each slice and roll it up into cannelloni. Place them seam-side down into a baking dish, pour over the tomato sauce, and sprinkle over the grated mozzarella and Parmesan cheese.

Bake for 10 to 15 minutes at 200 °C until hot and bubbling. Serve with a huge green salad and crusty bread to mop up the sauce!

SERVES 4

Savoury potato, roasted pepper and mushroom bake

For Edward Finn, my mad and adorable Irish friend, who would treat this as birthday cake he loves potatoes so much. Eddy the Tuber, I can understand how the Irish survived on potatoes!

- 1 kg peeled and cubed potatoes
- 100 g butter
- 300 g white button mushrooms, sliced
- 4 large onions, peeled and thinly sliced
- 2 cloves garlic, crushed
- 1 cup cream
- ½ teaspoon English mustard powder
- 3 eggs, beaten
- salt, to taste
- freshly ground black pepper
- pinch of nutmeg
- 4 red peppers, quartered, roasted and peeled
- 500 g wilted spinach, well drained
- 1 cup grated Gruyere cheese
- sliced red onion, for topping
- extra butter

Cook the potatoes till soft in lightly salted water; drain, mash and keep warm.

Heat half the butter in a frying pan and cook the mushrooms without salt; remove with a slotted spoon and set aside.

In the same pan heat the remaining butter till it foams and add the onions; cook without salt till they are lightly golden, then remove from the pan.

In the same pan add the garlic, cream and English mustard. Warm gently – do not boil – and scrape all the flavour off the bottom of the pan.

Mix together the potatoes and mushrooms, beaten egg and cream mixture, salt, pepper and nutmeg.

Spread one layer of mash onto the bottom of a well-buttered oven-proof dish and cover with the roasted peppers. Cover the peppers with the spinach and the remaining mash, and smooth down. Sprinkle the cheese over the top, arrange sliced onion over that and dot with a little extra butter.

Bake in the oven at 200 °C for about 20 minutes, or until the cheese is bubbling and golden.

Cut into portions and serve with a gorgeous big green salad of baby gem lettuce, rocket, red onion and Parmesan shavings, dressed with a nice, tart vinaigrette.

SERVES 4 – 6

TIP: This is a superb light vegetarian lunch, or it can be served as a side dish with meat, chicken or fish.

Did you know?

Potatoes are one of the world's most nutrient-dense foods. They contain folate, vitamins C, B1 and B6, fibre, iron, potassium, magnesium and lots of other minerals.

Buttery onion and asparagus tart

- 2 sheets frozen shortcrust pastry
- 40 g butter
- 2 onions, thinly sliced
- 1 cup grated mature cheddar cheese
- 3 tablespoons chopped fresh parsley
- 4 eggs, beaten
- 1 cup cream
- ½ cup milk
- a good pinch of nutmeg
- 1 tablespoon flour
- salt and pepper, to taste
- ½ cup snipped chives
- 12 green asparagus, steamed
- 100 g Fairview Chevin

Preheat the oven to 180 °C. Grease a 22 cm loose-bottomed flan tin, and line with the pastry; overlap the sheets and press them into the base and up the sides of the tin. Trim the edges neatly, allowing for some shrinkage, and chill for 30 minutes. (If you prefer, you can roll the pastry into a rectangular baking sheet.)

Remove from the fridge, line with greaseproof paper and pour in enough dry beans to cover the base of the tin. Bake the pastry blind for 10 minutes, then remove the paper and beans and set aside to cool completely.

Heat the butter and gently cook the onions till soft and golden. Let them cool completely, then spoon them onto the pastry base. Top with the cheddar cheese and the parsley.

Beat together the eggs, cream, milk, nutmeg, flour, salt, pepper and chives. Gently pour into the pastry case, arrange the asparagus on top and dot with slices of chevin.

Bake for 30 – 35 minutes at 180 °C or until set and golden. Serve with a fresh tomato salad dressed with basil pesto.

SERVES 4 – 6

No more soggy bottoms! While your oven is preheating, heat an oven tray and place your quiche tin onto that when it is ready to bake; this helps cook the bottom of the pastry.

Creamed baby onions and barley bake

THE ONIONS

- 500 g peeled baby onions
- 3 cloves
- 1 cup water
- 1 cup milk
- 1 cup cooked barley

THE SAUCE

- 3 tablespoons butter
- 3 tablespoons flour
- 1 teaspoon dry English mustard
- enough milk to make up 500 ml using the onion liquid
- 1 cup grated cheese of your choice
- salt and black pepper
- 1 teaspoon fresh thyme (or ½ teaspoon dried)
- ¾ cup fresh breadcrumbs

Place the peeled onions and the cloves in a saucepan and cover them with the water and milk. Simmer gently for about 15 minutes. Drain the onions, keeping the milk. Preheat the oven to 180 °C.

Now make the sauce. Melt the butter in a saucepan and stir in the flour and dried mustard. Cook gently until you have a nice smooth paste. Now slowly add 500 ml of onion-flavoured milk, whisking all the time. When the sauce is thick and smooth, add half the cheese and stir until it melts. Remove from the heat.

Stir in the barley and onions, season with salt and freshly ground black pepper, and spoon into a buttered baking dish.

Mix the remaining cheese and the thyme with the breadcrumbs, and scatter over the top of the onions. Bake at 180 °C for 20 to 25 minutes until golden and bubbling.

SERVES 4

TIP: I like to use Gruyere with onions. You can add mushrooms to this dish and slice tomatoes over the top.

Nut roast

- 200 g spinach, blanched and finely chopped
- 300 g roasted, unsalted mixed nuts, finely chopped
- ½ red onion, finely chopped
- 1 medium carrot, grated
- ½ cup chopped black olives
- ½ cup chopped sundried tomatoes
- 200 g canned tomatoes, drained and chopped
- 100 g grated Parmesan
- 1 cup grated halloumi cheese
- ½ cup chopped button mushrooms
- ½ cup chopped flat leaf parsley
- ¼ cup fresh basil
- 10 ml fresh thyme leaves
- 2 cloves garlic, crushed
- 1 beaten egg
- salt and black pepper

Preheat the oven to 180 °C. Place all the ingredients in a large mixing bowl and mix them together thoroughly. Have a little taste and adjust the seasoning if need be.

Butter a 1 kg bread baking tin well, and spoon the nut mixture into it. Press down firmly. Roast for about 1 hour, and let it rest in the tin for about 10 minutes before you turn it out.

Serve the nut loaf cut in slices with roasted veggies and a large salad.

SERVES 4

When cooking with sage be sure to choose nice fleshy leaves, firm green stalks and definitely not a sign of wilting or blemishes. It will be even more delicious if you pick it just before you need to use it.

Roasted butternut cheesecake with burnt sage butter

THE BASE
- 150 g savoury biscuit crumbs
- 100 g melted butter
- 1 teaspoon chopped rosemary needles

THE FILLING
- 500 g peeled butternut cubes
- 2 teaspoons olive oil
- 2 teaspoons rosemary needles
- salt
- pepper
- 1 teaspoon brown sugar
- 2 eggs, beaten
- 1 cup cream
- 300 g ricotta cheese
- 1 cup grated mature cheddar cheese
- ¼ teaspoon freshly grated nutmeg
- 2 cloves crushed garlic

SAGE BUTTER SAUCE
- 100 g butter
- 15 fresh, fleshy sage leaves

To prepare the base, mix the crumbs, butter and rosemary together. Press the mixture into a 20 cm springform baking tin, and set till firm in the fridge.

Make the filling next. Preheat the oven to 180 °C. Toss the butternut with the olive oil, rosemary, salt, pepper and sugar, and roast till tender; about 20 minutes. Remove from the oven and set aside.

Blend together the eggs, cream, ricotta, cheddar, nutmeg and garlic, and spoon over the biscuit base. Bake at 180 °C until set; approximately 35 to 40 minutes. Top with the roasted butternut.

Just before the cheesecake is ready to come out of the oven, prepare the sage butter sauce. Heat the butter in a pan until it begins to foam. Add the sage and cook until the butter starts to go nutty and brown, and the leaves are crisp.

Serve the cheesecake warm with some burnt sage butter, or cold with a large green salad.

SERVES 6 – 8

"Shipping is a terrible thing to do to vegetables. They probably get jet-lagged, just like people."
Elizabeth Berry

CHAPTER TWELVE

Something Extra
on the Side

My mother's cooking was homely, wholesome, nourishing and tasty. Her vegetables were always freshly bought or picked straight from our own garden, and her cooking was slow and mouth-watering, extracting every last drop of flavour so everything was deliciously merged. While I was growing up I got to eat some of the most amazingly fresh, organic produce I have ever tasted.

As a child, beans were one of my favourite vegetables. (In fact, they still are!) I loved topping and tailing the fresh beans we had just picked from the garden. I would get a tongue lashing for eating half of them before they even saw the pot and was sent back out to pick more.

I jumped off a roof once because my brother Billy told me I could have as many green beans from the garden as I wanted if I jumped off the top of the gardener's cottage. It wasn't that high, but my knees came up and hit me in the mouth. The blood flowed and we both got thrashed; but I got my beans so it was worth it!

Don't tail the beans here; it's a bit of sexiness from nature. I love the way their tails stand up in the dish!

Spiced green beans

- 1 tablespoon oil
- 1 teaspoon cumin seeds
- ¼ teaspoon coriander seeds
- ½ teaspoon mustard seeds
- ½ teaspoon smoked paprika
- ¼ teaspoon turmeric
- ½ teaspoon grated fresh ginger
- 2 cloves garlic, freshly crushed
- 1 tablespoon butter
- 1 kg baby beans, topped and blanched
- zest of 1 fresh lemon

Heat the oil in a large frying pan and add the seeds. Cook gently till they start to give you their divine scent; don't burn them, so keep them moving in the pan.

Now stir in the paprika, turmeric, ginger, garlic and butter. When the butter has melted, stir in the beans and lemon zest, and heat through.

Delicious served with roasts and stews as a side dish.

SERVES 4 – 6

TIP: You can turn this into a salad; toss the beans into half a cup of natural yoghurt and give them a splash of lemon juice.

Zesty almond-topped garlic green beans

- 3 tablespoons butter
- 2 cloves garlic, crushed
- zest of 2 ripe lemons
- 1.5 kg green beans
- salt and pepper to taste
- 100 g flaked almonds, toasted

Heat the butter in a saucepan and add the garlic and lemon zest.

Top and tail the beans and steam them lightly. Toss them into the flavoured butter and heat through. Season with salt and pepper, pile onto a heated platter and top with toasted almonds.

Delicious served with lamb or pork chops, and roasts.

SERVES 8

TIP: Don't be shy with the garlic or lemons, but keep the balance!

"In cooking, as in all arts,
simplicity is the sign of perfection."
Maurice Curnonsky

Cauliflower and toasted pine nuts

I sometimes serve this hot with chevin melted into the cauliflower; really yummy! It can also be served as a vegetarian meal – just add a couple of golden, crispy halloumi fingers.

- 1 small cauliflower, florets separated
- 40 g butter
- 40 g pine nuts
- 2 cloves garlic, peeled and finely chopped
- salt and freshly ground pepper
- extra virgin olive oil
- Parmesan cheese
- 2 tablespoons freshly chopped flat leaf parsley
- ground nutmeg

SERVES 4

Slice the cauliflower florets in half and set aside till you need them.

Heat the butter in a large frying pan and lightly brown the pine nuts; remove and set aside. Now add the garlic and cauliflower to the pan and cook gently, stirring every so often till just tender. Add a spoonful of water to create some steam if needed.

Season with salt and freshly ground black pepper, and stir in the pine nuts.

Transfer the cauliflower to a platter, drizzle with olive oil and cover with freshly grated Parmesan cheese and parsley. Add a good shake of nutmeg, toss together and serve. Delicious hot or cold, served with beef, pork and chicken dishes.

TIP: If you want a full and delicious nutmeg flavour, grate fresh nutmeg into your dish!

Baked leeks

I have a passion for leeks and grow huge beds of them in my garden – I use them young and tender, and big and swollen! I use them baked whole, or in salads, soups and stews. I like to harvest them when I need them so they are always in peak flavour.

- 12 young leeks, tops trimmed and washed
- 12 slices Parma ham or back bacon
- salt and black pepper
- 500 g roughly mashed new potatoes
- 1 cup freshly grated Gruyere cheese
- 1½ cups cream
- 2 teaspoons chopped rosemary
- 2 egg yolks
- ½ teaspoon ground nutmeg
- 1 tablespoon Parmesan
- 2 tablespoons fresh breadcrumbs

Place the leeks in a shallow pan of boiling water and cook for 6 minutes; remove and drain.

Lay the ham onto a flat surface, top each slice with a leek, season with salt and pepper, and wrap it up. Butter a baking dish large enough to hold the leeks, pile the potatoes onto the base, season and top with the leeks.

Mix the Gruyere cheese, cream, rosemary, egg yolks and nutmeg, and season to taste with salt and pepper. Pour over the leeks. Sprinkle over the Parmesan and breadcrumbs, and bake for 30 to 35 minutes, or until bubbling and golden.

Serve with a mixed baby leaf salad.

SERVES 4

"Anyone can count the seeds in an apple, but only God can count the number of apples in a seed." Robert H. Schuller

Apple-braised red cabbage

- 2 tablespoons olive oil
- star anise
- ½ teaspoon caraway seeds
- 1 red onion, sliced
- 2 green apples, chopped
- 1 teaspoon chopped ginger
- 3 tablespoons apple juice
- ½ cup sultanas
- 2 tablespoons balsamic vinegar
- 1 tablespoon brown sugar
- 3 cups shredded red cabbage

Heat the olive oil, and add the star anise and the caraway seeds, frying for 30 seconds. Then add the onion, apples and ginger, and cook for 6 minutes.

Add the apple juice, sultanas, balsamic vinegar, brown sugar and cabbage, and cook till the cabbage is tender.

Delicious served with roast pork, pork chops, pork schnitzel and lamb chops.

SERVES 4–6

Honeyed sweet potatoes

I think that sweet potatoes must be an almost perfect food. They are wonderfully nutritious, full of fibre, vitamins and minerals, and are a great source of beta-carotene. They are also low in fat and contain no cholesterol. I serve them to my family at least once a week, be it baked, roasted, steamed or stir-fried; they are even delicious thinly sliced and tossed in an orange and fresh coriander vinaigrette.

- 4 nice, clean medium-large sweet potatoes
- 3 tablespoons brandy or Van der Hum
- 1 tablespoon brown sugar
- 1 tablespoon runny honey
- peel of 1 orange without pith, shredded
- 80 g butter
- salt and pepper
- ground cinnamon

Boil the sweet potatoes unpeeled and whole in salted water till they are fork tender. Drain, slice the potatoes thickly and arrange in an oven-proof dish. Sprinkle with brandy and brown sugar, drizzle with honey, scatter on the orange peel and dot with butter. Season with salt and pepper, and dust with cinnamon.

Bake at 180 °C for 20 minutes or until the top starts to caramelise. Serve as an accompaniment to any roast, especially roast lamb.

SERVES 4

"There are five elements: earth, air, fire, water and garlic." *Louis Diat*

I love garlic and really don't mind carrying the evidence on my breath! Why do we get hysterical about it in our food? We need to wake up now ... sing its praises. I really don't give a fig about it making my breath smell when I know it can lower my risk of colon cancer, that it promotes good circulation and lowers cholesterol, and that it has antibacterial properties. These are just a few of the wonderful health benefits you will get from garlic; eaten raw the benefits are even greater.

I always add it to my dressings and stir a few crushed cloves of fresh garlic into my stews, soups, pastas and curries just before serving. It adds body and a depth of flavour.

Roasting garlic mellows it; it takes away that strong, pungent flavour that many people find offensive. Prepare yourself for a treat! The sweet, nutty flesh of the garlic cloves is transformed to a fragrant paste – ooze it all over your meat, or scrape it onto toast drizzled with some fine extra virgin olive oil, and add some sea salt and a healthy grind of black pepper. Just try it!

Roasted garlic

Roasted garlic makes a wonderful side dish to serve alongside a lamb or beef roast, and it is also good with chicken.

- plump, firm bulbs of garlic
- a few sprigs of fresh rosemary
- extra virgin olive oil
- black pepper
- seaweed or sea salt

Preheat the oven to 180 °C. Allowing one full garlic bulb per person, cut the top off the bulbs to expose the cloves inside.

Cut squares of tin foil to the size of each bulb with enough to fold around and cover the bulb securely, and place a sprig of rosemary on the base of the foil. Place the garlic bulb onto the rosemary and give it a drizzle of extra virgin olive, a good grind of black pepper and a sprinkle of salt.

Close up the foil and bake the garlic parcel for about 35 to 40 minutes depending on the size of the bulbs.

Serve a parcel to each person.

"There is no such thing as a little garlic."
Arthur Baer

Green onion mashed potatoes

Nobody makes a mash like my little Marga; her mash is smooth and tasty and she puts a lot of love into the pot!

- 4 medium potatoes, peeled
- 80 ml butter
- 4 cloves garlic, crushed (yes, 4!)
- 80 ml full cream milk, or cream
- 2 spring onions with tops, finely chopped
- 1 small handful Italian parsley, chopped
- pinch of freshly grated nutmeg

Place the potatoes into a suitably-sized pot, cover with cold salted water and bring to the boil. Cook until tender, and then strain into a colander.

Melt the butter in a pan with the garlic. Once the garlic is fragrant, gently stir in the milk or cream (or half each), spring onions, parsley and nutmeg, and remove from the heat.

Always mash the potatoes while warm, adding the warm milk mixture gradually to the potatoes as you mash them. Make sure that you remove all lumps. Season well with salt and pepper and add a little more milk or butter if necessary. Taste, adjust the seasoning and if you are like me you will be stirring in more butter and milk.

This is particularly good served with pork schnitzel. I love to stir freshly chopped dill, deep-fried capers, a little garlic, spring onion and lemon zest into my mash for serving with fish!

SERVES 4

TIP: You can stir in finely chopped sautéed mushrooms, chopped sundried tomatoes or bacon bits. In fact, you can add anything that would complement your dish; just take care to adjust the liquid and butter.

I love this potato cake hot or cold! It makes a delicious light meal served with a green salad, and it is a wonderful picnic dish. It is also the perfect accompaniment to a simple dish of fried chicken. Be sure to add the salty anchovies; they add another layer of flavour to this tasty dish!

Potato cake with a hint of the Mediterranean

THE POTATOES

- 1 kg potatoes, unpeeled
- 2 tablespoons butter
- 1 tablespoon olive oil
- 2 onions, thinly sliced
- 3 leeks, white part only, sliced
- 4 cloves garlic, chopped
- 1 tablespoon chopped fresh thyme leaves
- 5 anchovy fillets, chopped
- 150 g sliced salami
- 5 tablespoons basil pesto
- freshly ground black pepper

THE TOP

- freshly grated Parmesan cheese
- 1 red onion, sliced
- sprigs of fresh thyme
- 10 black olives
- ½ cup cream
- salt and pepper
- butter for dotting

SERVES 4 – 6

Boil the potatoes for 7 minutes till just tender. Cool and slice thickly.

Gently heat the butter and olive oil in a pan and cook the onions and leeks for 4 minutes; season with lots of black pepper. Stir in the garlic and thyme and cook for another 2 minutes. Remove from the heat and stir in the anchovies.

Butter a 20 cm cake tin with a loose bottom and arrange a third of the potatoes onto the base of the tin. Top with half the onion mix, then half the salami, and dot with half the pesto. Cover with another third of the potatoes and the rest of the onions, salami and pesto. Give it a good grind of black pepper. Arrange the remaining sliced potatoes over the salami and onions.

Now top it with the grated Parmesan. Arrange the sliced red onion onto the cheese and scatter with sprigs of fresh thyme and black olives. Lastly, season the cream lightly and pour it over the top. Dot with butter and bake for 1 hour at 190 °C.

When the cake is done, cool a while and remove from the tin. Serve warm with extra pesto and a drizzle of extra virgin olive oil. Be sure to have a huge bowl of rocket, red onions and cos lettuce tossed with lemon vinaigrette on the side.

TIP: Always cook potatoes in cold, salted water. As potatoes require a relatively long cooking time, this allows for more even cooking and heat penetration from the outside to the inside.

I can't imagine not being able to cook with onions – they are the foundation of so many dishes. I am sure that onions are cultivated in every country on Earth. According to an old wives' tale, a cut onion will attract all infections flying around in the air and kill them; so not a bad idea to leave a few onion halves in a corner of the room!

Raw or cooked, onions not only give you flavour, but they have wonderful health-promoting properties too. They are high in antioxidants, so if you have flu, infuse some sliced onion in boiling water and let it steep for a while. Eat the onion, stir some honey into the onion water and drink it.

Did you know that red onions are rich in the flavonoid quercetin which is thought to be one of the most powerful cardio-protective substances yet discovered? I will be eating my fair share of red onions for the rest of my natural life!

Honey baked red onions

I love to make these delicious baked onions often; the roasting makes them so sweet, sticky and wonderfully caramelised. They are a great side dish with almost anything and wonderful on a toasted ciabatta topped with cream cheese for a quick lunch!

- 4 large red onions
- ½ cup balsamic vinegar
- 2 tablespoons olive oil
- honey for drizzling
- salt
- freshly ground black pepper

Preheat the oven to 200 °C. Leaving the skins on and roots intact, cut the onions into quarters and place them in a baking dish. Shake together the balsamic vinegar and olive oil and spoon onto the onions. Now drizzle with honey and season with salt and freshly ground black pepper.

Roast on the middle shelf of the oven for 20 minutes; remove from the oven and gently toss the onions in the pan juices. Serve hot or cold with roast beef or lamb, or fried lamb's liver.

SERVES 4 – 6

"Life is an onion and one cries while peeling it."
French proverb

This is delicious served with best-quality sausages perched on top. Sizzling and spitting sausages go in the pan limp and pink, and as the heat gets to them they start to swell and take on a gorgeous golden brown hue. You can see the juices bubbling under the skin and they say, 'Eat me, eat me,' and I do!

New potato rarebit

- 25 g butter
- 6 rashers streaky bacon, finely chopped (optional)
- 1 medium onion, diced
- 3 medium leeks, washed and diced
- 1 ½ cups beer
- 225 g grated Gruyere cheese
- 125 g grated mature cheddar
- 1 tablespoon cornflour
- 2 tablespoons milk
- 1 teaspoon Dijon mustard
- 1 teaspoon Worcestershire sauce
- pinch of smoked paprika
- salt and pepper to taste
- 1 kg new potatoes, boiled till tender
- 1 teaspoon fresh thyme leaves

Preheat the oven to 180 °C. Place the butter in a saucepan and melt it; now stir in the bacon. Add the onion and leeks, and cook till they have softened nicely. Add the beer and bring to the boil, then add the cheeses and stir till they are melted.

Mix the cornflour and milk together till smooth and stir into the cheeses with the mustard, Worcestershire sauce, paprika, salt and pepper. Cook for 2 minutes.

Place the potatoes in a baking dish, squash them with your thumb and pour over the rarebit. Scatter with thyme and bake till hot, golden and bubbling!

SERVES 4 – 6

I normally choose a medium-sized potato for this dish, because I like to serve one and a half to two potatoes per person, especially when my friend Jeff Wittels comes for dinner because he just loves my roast potatoes. But my biggest potato fan is Imran Khan – these are for you, my darling!

Roasted rosemary lemony potatoes for Imran

- 8 medium potatoes, boiled with skin on till just tender
- 1 large ripe juicy lemon
- olive oil
- salt and freshly ground black pepper
- lots of freshly chopped rosemary
- 1 teaspoon cumin seeds

Preheat the oven to 190 °C. Slice the potatoes lengthways into two and peel the skins off. Place them onto an oven tray, squeeze over the lemon juice and drizzle liberally with olive oil. Season with salt and pepper, and scatter over the rosemary and the cumin seeds.

Roast till crisp, for about 45 to 55 minutes, turning a few times if needed.

SERVES 4

Bacon and butternut mash

This makes a delicious side dish, or you can use it to stuff cannelloni or ravioli. Ring the changes and use sage or rosemary instead of thyme, but beware – they are strong herbs so use them sparingly; you don't want to lose the wonderful flavour of the butternut.

- 1.5 kg peeled butternut, chopped
- 4 young leeks sliced
- 1 tablespoon fresh thyme leaves
- butter
- 1 clove fresh garlic, crushed
- 150 g mascarpone cheese
- 1 cup crispy, chopped streaky bacon
- freshly ground black pepper
- salt, to taste

Gently steam the butternut till it is just cooked; drain and return to the pot.

Gently fry the leeks and thyme in a little butter; don't brown them, keep them soft and tender.

Mash together the butternut, leeks, garlic and mascarpone. Stir through the bacon, and season with salt and lots of freshly ground black pepper.

Pile onto hot plates with the rest of what you are serving – particularly good with big, fat, juicy sausages or under a juicy pork chop.

SERVES 4–6

TIP: Choose butternuts that have long firm necks and small bottoms; makes sense, why pay for a big hollow bottom full of pips?

Brussels sprouts, baby tomatoes and bacon

- 250 g Brussels sprouts
- 3 rashers streaky bacon, finely chopped
- 2 teaspoons fresh thyme leaves
- 2 leeks, white part only, sliced and washed
- 3 cloves peeled garlic, finely chopped
- 200 g Rosa tomatoes
- 125 ml fresh cream (optional)
- seaweed salt or sea salt
- freshly ground black pepper
- 3 tablespoons freshly snipped chives
- 1 tablespoon butter
- shavings of Parmesan cheese

I love Brussels sprouts, whether lightly steamed and tossed in butter with a dusting of freshly grated nutmeg, grated Parmesan and salt and pepper, or cooked in one of hundreds of other ways. They are just delicious!

Trim and wash the Brussels sprouts and steam lightly.

Heat a frying pan and gently cook the fat out of the bacon. Then add the thyme and leeks, stirring until the leeks start to wilt. (If you can't get any fresh thyme, you can use 1 teaspoon of dried thyme instead – rub it between your fingers when you add it to the pan.) Add the garlic and cook for 1 minute.

Add the Brussels sprouts and tomatoes, and cook till the tomatoes start to wrinkle. Stir in the cream now if you are using it, and cook for a minute. Add some salt and pepper, stir in the chives and butter, spoon into a dish and top with Parmesan shavings. Yum!

SERVES 4

My family just adores carrots, cooked or raw. Where most would eat 100 g each as part of a balanced meal, I need to cook 1.5 kg for my family of five and they disappear from the pot before they even reach the table!

Thyme for carrots

- 6 large carrots, peeled and cut into rings
- 3 peeled potatoes, quartered
- 1 large onion, finely chopped
- 4 cloves garlic, peeled
- 2 teaspoons fresh thyme leaves
- 80 – 100 g salted butter
- ¼ cup milk
- salt and white pepper

Place the carrots, potatoes, onion and garlic in a saucepan. Cover with cold water, add salt, bring to the boil, and cook till the potatoes are tender. Strain and return immediately to the pot.

Add the thyme, butter and milk and roughly mash together; taste and adjust the seasoning. Please feel free to add extra butter!

Serve with whatever takes your fancy.

SERVES 4

Bacon, beans and sage

You can pre-soak some dried beans overnight if you wish, or you can use them from the can; no shame in that, just gets it to your mouth quicker. The sharp, salty flavour of the crispy bacon works so well with the beans and sage.

- 1½ tablespoons unsalted butter
- 250 g streaky bacon, chopped
- 5 fresh sage leaves
- 4 garlic cloves, crushed
- 1 large leek, finely sliced
- 400 g can chopped tomatoes
- salt
- freshly ground black pepper
- 2 cans butter beans, drained

Heat a tablespoon of the butter in a frying pan and fry the bacon slowly till crisp; remove the bacon from the pan. Fry the sage leaves in the bacon fat till crisp. Remove the sage and set aside. Drain off a little of the bacon fat.

To the same pan add the garlic and leek slices, and cook till the leeks are wilted; about 4 minutes. Add the tomatoes and season with salt and pepper. Cook for 6 minutes, then stir in the butter beans and remaining butter. Heat the beans through and stir in the bacon and crushed sage leaves.

Serve hot as beans on toast or as a side dish with pork chops or sausages. If you have any leftovers, serve them for breakfast topped with a soft poached egg.

SERVES 4–6

Spanish-style chickpeas

Whether you call them garbanzo beans, Bengal gram or chickpeas, these healthy pulses are high in protein and are really good for you. It is said that they were already being cultivated in the Middle East about 7500 years ago, making them one of the earliest vegetables to be grown. Not only do they have a long history, but they are delicious too. That works for me!

- 2 tablespoons olive oil
- 1 large onion, chopped
- 1 teaspoon smoked paprika
- 4 cloves garlic, chopped
- 3 cups cooked chickpeas
- 1 large red pepper, roasted and chopped
- 1 large yellow pepper, roasted and chopped
- 1 large ripe tomato, chopped
- salt and black pepper
- 2 tablespoons roughly chopped coriander
- 2 tablespoons roughly chopped flat leaf parsley
- ½ cup chopped black olives

Heat the olive oil and gently cook the onion down till it is soft. Add the smoked paprika, garlic and chickpeas, and cook, stirring till the chickpeas are coated with the paprika. Stir in the roasted peppers and tomato, and cook for 5 minutes.

Season to taste, and stir in the chopped coriander, parsley and olives.

Delicious served with roast chicken, steaks and chops. Or try them roughly mashed under a juicy piece of steamed fish, or even served as a warm salad.

SERVES 4

"An empty belly is the best cook."
Estonian proverb

CHAPTER THIRTEEN

Oh, you *Saucy* Thing!

When I was growing up, I loved the stories my mother used to tell about my grandmother and her famous green fingers.

Everything my grandmother planted flourished. So much so that one day she lost her wedding ring in the parsley patch. They searched and searched for months, but they couldn't find it because the parsley grew so thick and fast and lush you couldn't even see to the bottom of it. Of course, with parsley the more you pick, the more it grows, and my granny used to supply the local butcher and fishmonger. It was only years later when they turned the beds over that they found her ring.

Listening to these stories, I knew that when I grew up I too would want a garden of my own, from which I could pick a salad, or some fragrant herbs to flavour a sauce or stew.

I am lucky enough to have my own vegetable garden now, and it gives me such pleasure. This is what I love – the flavour and the texture of freshly picked ingredients. It's like living food.

I would like to share a few sauces and dressings with you that you could use on just about anything – nude noodles, fish, meat, chicken, salad – you name it. They are all great for dipping and spooning and splashing over food!

Homemade aïoli

- 2 fat garlic cloves
- 2 fresh egg yolks
- 200 ml sunflower oil
- 100 ml extra virgin olive oil
- lemon juice, to taste
- salt, to taste
- freshly ground black pepper
- zest of a small, ripe lemon (optional)

Aïoli is a great French classic. You can use this garlicky mayonnaise for absolutely anything; good with fish, seafood, asparagus and new potatoes or as a dip for crudités, to name but a few!

Pound the garlic to a paste with a little salt; transfer to a clean bowl. Now whisk the egg yolks into the garlic paste.

Add the oil slowly now, a drop at a time, until you have used up half the oil. Add a teaspoon of lemon juice and continue to add the remaining oil, in a slow, steady drizzle. Taste, adjust the seasoning, stir in the lemon zest if you are using it, and chill.

MAKES ABOUT 350 ml

TIP: Use it up on the same day because it is made with raw eggs!

Cheat's lime and chilli aïoli

- ¾ cup really good-quality mayonnaise
- 1 tablespoon finely grated lime rind
- 2½ tablespoons freshly squeezed lime juice
- 2 cloves garlic, mashed
- 1 small red chilli, diced
- 1 tablespoon freshly chopped coriander

It doesn't hurt to jazz up a commercial mayonnaise, so long as you use a good-quality one. You can make it work as a topping or sauce for so many different dishes.

Stir all the ingredients together till well combined and transfer to a pretty bowl.

MAKES ABOUT 1 CUP

Chilli and garlic aïoli

- 1 cup homemade mayonnaise, or the best you can buy
- 3 cloves garlic, mashed to a paste
- 1 teaspoon lime zest
- 2 teaspoons ripe lemon zest
- 2 green chillies, finely chopped
- 1 tablespoon fresh lemon juice
- salt, to taste
- freshly ground black pepper

Delicious on fish, potato wedges and poached chicken – actually, on almost everything!

Mix all the ingredients together and chill for at least an hour before you need it – let those flavours become well acquainted. Use lavishly.

SERVES 4–6

TIP: Always use ripe lemons; unripe lemons are bitter and will spoil your dish.

Preserved lemon dressing

- 2 tablespoons capers, deep-fried and chopped
- ½ preserved lemon rind, finely chopped
- ½ cup roughly chopped flat leaf parsley
- ½ cup chopped mint
- 6 tablespoons olive oil
- zest of 1 ripe lemon
- ½ cup freshly squeezed lemon juice
- 1 clove garlic, crushed
- salt and black pepper

I love this spooned over a thick fillet of poached fish or a fried skate wing. Or on a chunk of seared tuna!

Shake it all up together and spoon over grilled or poached fish.

MAKES 1½ CUPS

My lemon and herb salad dressing

- 2 cloves garlic
- ½ teaspoon salt
- 1 teaspoon English mustard powder
- 2 tablespoons red wine vinegar
- ½ cup fresh mint
- ½ cup parsley, with stems
- 2 tablespoons lemon juice
- 1 tablespoon honey
- 2 teaspoons lemon zest
- ½ cup olive oil
- 1 tablespoon olive oil

I normally make three times more than I need of this dressing and keep it in the fridge. I use it over a few days; we have a fresh salad every night with our meal.

Give it all a whizz in a blender. Taste and adjust the flavour with salt, lemon juice or olive oil. Perfect for drizzling over your favourite salad.

ENOUGH FOR 1 SALAD

TIP: I like to use a lemon-infused olive oil for this dressing.

Minty caper and parsley dressing

- 2 tablespoons baby capers
- 1 chilli
- 2 tablespoons red onion
- 3 tablespoons Italian parsley
- 3 tablespoons coriander
- 2 cloves garlic, crushed
- 2 tablespoons lemon juice
- 4 tablespoons olive oil
- 2 tablespoons chopped mint
- salt and black pepper

I love to spoon this over fried fish or calamari. It is delicious stirred into crushed boiled potatoes or lentils, and makes a great dressing for a bean salad.

Finely chop the chilli, red onion, Italian parsley and coriander. Shake it all up in a jar to blend, adjust the seasoning and serve.

SERVES 4

Portly cranberry sauce

- 200 g sundried cranberries
- 400 ml port
- juice and rind of 1 orange
- juice and rind of 1 ripe lemon
- 1 tablespoon vegetable oil
- 6 cm fresh ginger, peeled and cut into thin strips
- 1 cup sugar
- 1 dried red chilli
- 1 clove garlic, crushed
- salt
- a good grind of Sichuan pepper
- a pinch of ground cloves

I love to serve this flavourful, fruity sauce with game, ostrich or gammon. It is also good with beef, pork, chicken and lamb.

Soak the cranberries in the port with the citrus juice and the zest for 30 minutes.

Heat a little oil in a saucepan and gently fry the ginger till it is lightly golden. Add the sugar and chilli, and stir well into the ginger. Add the cranberries and garlic, and cook gently till reduced by a third. Taste the sauce and season with salt, Sichuan pepper and cloves.

Keep this bottled in the fridge till you need it; it keeps well. Serve cold as a relish or hot with roasted meats.

MAKES ABOUT 400 ml

Lime and coriander dressing

- 2 fat cloves garlic, peeled
- 2 large green chillies (2 more for the brave at heart)
- ½ cup chopped fresh coriander
- 1 tablespoon fish sauce
- 1 tablespoon palm sugar
- 4 spring onions with tops, chopped
- ½ cup freshly squeezed lime juice
- 1 teaspoon finely chopped fresh ginger
- 1 stem lemon grass, tender part pounded
- ½ cup fresh sweet basil

This dressing is particularly good with all leafy salad greens or slaw. It is wonderful spooned over grilled fish or noodle salads, and makes a great dipping sauce for steamed prawns.

Fling everything into a blender and blend for a minute. Store in a jar and refrigerate till needed.

SERVES 4

You can't beat freshly-made mint sauce. I can't believe how many of my friends use a bottled sauce; this is for you, my darlings!

Mint sauce

- 1 cup, tightly packed fresh mint
- 50 g sugar
- 100 ml boiling water
- 50 ml malt vinegar
- a little extra mint, chopped

Place the mint and sugar in a blender and give it a good whizz. Add the boiling water and blend again. Add the vinegar and give it another whizz. Pour into your serving bowl or jug, and stir in the extra chopped mint.

MAKES 1 CUP

TIP: There is nothing better than freshly-made mint sauce served with succulent, tender roast lamb. It will last for a few days if kept in the fridge.

Horseradish cream

- 3 tablespoons freshly grated horseradish
- 1½ tablespoons white wine vinegar
- 1 teaspoon castor sugar
- 1 cup cream, lightly whipped
- salt, to taste

The one thing I have been blessed with is an abundance of fresh horseradish growing in my garden. This delicious, sinus-clearing herb spreads like wild fire and I am glad, because there is nothing better than a sauce made from freshly grated horseradish!

Mix the horseradish, vinegar and sugar together. Stir into the whipped cream, taste and season with salt. Allow the horseradish cream to infuse for an hour before using it. Spoon onto roast beef and steaks.

SERVES 4 – 6

TIP: If you are brave enough, you can add a bit more horseradish to the cream!

Parsley and rocket pesto

- 1 clove garlic, peeled
- ½ cup rocket
- 1 cup flat leaf parsley
- 3 tablespoons freshly grated Parmesan cheese
- 3 tablespoons olive oil
- 1 ½ tablespoons freshly squeezed lemon juice
- 1 tablespoon lemon zest
- salt, to taste
- freshly ground black pepper

These two herbs grow like wild fire in my garden and I love nothing better than pounding or blending the two together into a pesto in the summer. Just before winter comes, I make a large batch and freeze it so that I can enjoy summer in winter! (Only add the cheese when you are about to serve it.)

Place all the ingredients in a blender and blend together till smooth. Season to taste. Use as you would a basil pesto. Delicious on sandwiches and stirred into pasta, or add a large blob of butter and stir it into crushed, boiled potatoes.

SERVES 4

Quick-fix peanut sauce

- 2 cloves garlic
- 8 tablespoons peanut butter
- 1 red chilli, chopped
- 2 teaspoons palm sugar
- 1 teaspoon fish sauce
- 1 x 400 ml can coconut milk
- 1 stem lemon grass, chopped
- 2 teaspoons chopped fresh ginger
- ½ teaspoon sesame oil
- small handful chopped coriander
- 3 large basil leaves, rolled and sliced at the last minute
- zest and juice of 1 lime
- salt, to taste

Wonderful on beef, pork or chicken kebabs; also good as a condiment to serve with roast pork.

Blitz together the garlic, peanut butter, chilli, palm sugar, fish sauce, coconut milk, lemon grass and ginger in a blender.

Transfer the sauce to a saucepan and simmer until reduced by a third. Stir in the sesame oil, coriander, basil, lime zest and juice. Taste, adjust the seasoning and serve!

MAKES ABOUT 400 ml

Orange and soy sauce

- 2 tablespoons peanut oil
- 1 tablespoon toasted coriander seeds, crushed
- 1 tablespoon toasted fennel seeds, crushed
- 1 tablespoon toasted cumin seeds, crushed
- 2 sticks cinnamon, broken
- 4 star anise
- 120 ml soy sauce
- 2 tablespoons fish sauce
- very thinly sliced rind of 1 orange, cut into strips
- juice of 2 oranges
- 1 thumb-sized piece of fresh ginger, cut into thin matchsticks
- 3 tablespoons runny honey
- 1 tablespoon brown sugar
- 1 red chilli, sliced
- ½ teaspoon ground white pepper

This sauce is delicious spooned over pork, duck and beef, or reduced further and painted onto beef at the end of roasting.

Heat the oil in a small saucepan and stir in the coriander, fennel and cumin seeds.

Then add the cinnamon and star anise and fry for 1 minute, stirring.

Add the remaining ingredients and simmer gently till reduced by half. Serve hot.

SERVES 4

Yakitori sauce

- 1 tablespoon peanut oil
- 3 cm fresh ginger, peeled and cut into matchsticks
- 4 cloves garlic, peeled and roughly chopped
- 6 tablespoons light soy sauce
- 8 tablespoons chicken or fish stock
- 3 tablespoons brown sugar
- 1 tablespoon honey
- 5 tablespoons white wine
- 3 tablespoons sweet sherry
- 2 spring onions with tops, thinly sliced
- 1 red chilli, diced (optional)
- 1 tablespoon chopped coriander
- 1 tablespoon chopped mint

Heat the oil in a small saucepan and add the ginger and garlic. Cook, stirring for about 2 minutes; do not burn. Add the remaining ingredients and cook gently till the sauce reduces and is nice and syrupy.

Serve with seafood, deep-fried calamari, or spooned over fried fish or poached chicken. A great sauce to have around!

SERVES 4

"A good appetite is the best sauce."
Anonymous

228

Roasted red pepper and almond sauce

- 3 large roasted red peppers
- 1 cup blanched almonds, toasted in a dry pan
- 4 cloves garlic, peeled
- 1 teaspoon cumin seeds, toasted
- ¼ cup extra virgin olive oil
- ½ cup coriander
- ½ cup flat leaf parsley
- ¼ teaspoon ground cinnamon
- salt and pepper, to taste

Blitz all the ingredients together in a blender till smooth. Serve on crisp rounds of crostini, or heat it gently and serve as a topping for poached fish or chicken.

SERVES 4 – 6

Honey ginger dipping sauce

- ½ cup soy sauce
- 3 tablespoons black Chinese vinegar, or balsamic
- 1 tablespoon chopped ginger
- 2 cloves garlic, crushed
- 1 teaspoon sesame oil
- 1 tablespoon vegetable oil
- 2 teaspoons runny honey
- 1 red chilli, sliced
- 1 spring onion, thinly sliced
- 1 tablespoon roughly chopped fresh coriander

As much as I call this a dipping sauce, it makes a delicious dressing for a red cabbage and sprout salad. I even spoon some onto cooked noodles and it works beautifully drizzled over crushed baby potatoes.

Place all the ingredients in a jar with a tight-fitting lid and give it a good shake. Any leftover sauce will keep in the fridge for a few days.

SERVES 4

Mango salsa

- 1 medium red onion, diced
- 1 red chilli, thinly sliced
- zest of 2 limes
- 1 teaspoon toasted cumin seeds, roughly ground
- ½ cup chopped coriander
- juice of 2 limes
- 1 tablespoon olive oil
- 1 teaspoon grated ginger
- 1 large clove garlic, crushed
- salt and pepper
- 1 large ripe mango, peeled and diced

Great with fish and seafood dishes, pork and chicken!

Stir all the ingredients together, except the mango. Once everything is well mixed, gently stir in the mango – take care not to mush it!

SERVES 4

"A world without tomatoes is like a string quartet without violins." *Laurie Colwin*

Sweet chilli tomato sauce

- 2 tablespoons peanut oil
- 1 red onion, thinly sliced
- 2 red chillies, seeded and sliced
- 30 g fresh ginger, finely chopped
- 6 cloves garlic, finely chopped
- 6 really ripe tomatoes, skinned, seeded and finely chopped
- 2 tablespoons fish sauce
- 1 tablespoon sugar

Heat the oil in a saucepan, add the onion, chillies, ginger and garlic, and cook till wonderfully fragrant. Stir in the tomatoes, fish sauce and sugar. Lower the heat and simmer till it reduces and is thick and chunky; add half a cup of water if it looks like it might stick. Serve warm with fish cakes.

MAKES ABOUT 2 CUPS

CHAPTER FOURTEEN

Knead me!

Because of Mrs Niemand and her boarding house with its coal stove and litchi trees in the garden, I have a passion for freshly baked breads.

I was about five years old when I first tasted her bread, but can remember it vividly to this day, and still feel the crust against my teeth.

The boarding house had lots of rooms, and they used to serve tea to their guests in the mornings. Her granddaughter Annekie was my best friend and the two of us would help her granny by going upstairs and bringing the tea trays down for her. After the trays went to the scullery, Mrs Niemand would sit us down at her enormous dining room table where she would reward us with huge slabs of her freshly baked bread.

It had a light, bubbly texture and a dark, crisp and crunchy crust. It was divine – spread with thick, chilled butter and homemade apricot jam, that was sticky and sweet and sour with chunks of fruit, and even a few kernels that tasted of almonds.

I swore that one day when I was a big girl with a family of my own I would give them nothing else to eat but bread and apricot jam.

I've never been able to recreate Mrs Niemand's luscious loaves, but I can bake bread – and so can you.

"Bread is the warmest, kindest of all words. Write it always with a capital letter, like your own name."

From a café sign

Jenny's basic bread dough

This is a wonderful dough; you can use it to make pizza, flat breads, rolls or bread sticks, and you can shape it any way you like.

- 4 cups cake flour
- 2 teaspoons salt
- 4 teaspoons sugar
- 10 g instant yeast
- 1 tablespoon olive oil (sunflower will do)
- 400 ml lukewarm water

Place all the dry ingredients into a bowl and make a well in the centre. Add the oil and three quarters of the water, and mix it in to form a soft dough. Add a little more water if need be; if it is too wet, add a small amount of flour.

Knead the dough until it is smooth and elastic to the touch; about 15 minutes. Place the dough back into the bowl and oil the top; cover with a clean cloth and place it in a warm place to rise to twice its size.

Remove the dough from the bowl, and shape and fill it any way you would like.

If you want to bake your daily bread, this recipe will yield 2 medium-sized loaves. Grease the loaf tins well with butter and dust with flour. Divide the dough between the loaf tins; cover and leave in a warm place to rise to twice their size.

Bake at 200 °C for 35 to 45 minutes. Invert the tin, slide out the loaf and tap it on the bottom. If it sounds hollow, the bread is ready to come out of the oven. If not, pop it back in straight onto the oven rack and let it bake for a few more minutes.

MAKES 2 LOAVES

Flat bread

Make a batch of Jenny's basic bread dough. Once the dough has risen to twice its size in the bowl, turn it out onto a floured surface, knock it down and shape it into a long oval loaf. Place it onto a floured baking sheet and top it with chunks of feta cheese, wedges or rings of red onions, cherry tomatoes, black olives and fresh rosemary. If you happen to have a few olive leaves, press them into the dough. Sprinkle a little white flour over the toppings.

Make sure that you push the toppings deep into the dough so that they don't pop out when the dough rises for the second time.

Let the flat bread rise to twice its size and then bake it for 45 to 50 minutes at 200 °C. Once the bread has baked and has a hollow sound when tapped on the bottom, cool it on a baking rack before serving.

"Blues is to jazz what yeast is to bread. Without it, it's flat."
Carmen McRae

Bread Tips

- Use a sharp, floured knife to cut patterns onto your bread dough before baking.
- Lightly oil a terracotta flowerpot and make flowerpot loaves – a small one needs to bake for about 25 minutes at 190 °C.
- If you are freezing dough, increase the quantity of yeast by a third.
- My mother uses saved unsalted potato water to make her bread; it gives it extra flavour!

Big fat cheese rolls

- **1 batch of Jenny's basic bread dough**
- **½ cup soft butter**
- **1 cup grated cheese**

Mix up a batch of Jenny's basic bread dough according to the instructions on page 234. Once the dough has doubled in size, remove it from the bowl, punch it down and roll out into a rectangle the size of a small chopping board.

On the first third of the dough, spread half of the butter and sprinkle with half of the cheese. Fold the dough over and do it again, and then roll it up into a Swiss roll shape.

Roll it up and down on a flat, floured surface till it is a little longer, and then cut it into 8 pieces. Press them down onto a well-oiled baking sheet, and let them rise again to twice their size.

Preheat the oven to 200 °C. Place the rolls into the oven and bake for 20 minutes till golden and bubbling. If after 20 minutes they are still a little pale, leave for a few more minutes. Remove and cool on a wire rack.

You may also like to try the following fillings:
- Cherry tomatoes, olives, rosemary, feta, bacon
- Cinnamon and butter
- Pesto

MAKES 8 LARGE OR 10 MEDIUM CHEESE ROLLS

"Nothing can go very far wrong at the table as long as there is honest bread, butter, olive oil, a generous spirit, lively appetites and attention to what we are eating."
Sybille Bedford

Desert bread

I have given this the name of desert bread because when I ate it in Morocco our guide said that they made it in the desert. The bulgur wheat gave it extra body and made it last longer on desert tours. I loved it, so here is my twist on it!

- 3 ½ cups cake flour
- 1 cup pre-soaked bulgur wheat
- 10 g yeast
- 2 teaspoons salt
- 4 teaspoons sugar
- about 1 ½ cups water
- extra flour or ½ cup polenta, for sprinkling

Preheat the oven to 180 °C. Mix all the dry ingredients together in a bowl. Gradually add the water until the mixture is pliable enough to knead into bread dough; add a little more water if needed. Knead the dough until it is soft and put it in an oiled bowl.

Cover the bowl, put it in a warm place and proof the dough for 40 minutes, or until nicely risen. Gently knead the dough and shape into round, flat breads.

Sprinkle with the polenta and allow it to rise again for about 30 minutes, or until nice and puffy. Bake for 25 to 30 minutes or until golden brown.

MAKES 6–8 LITTLE FLAT BREADS

Beat it and bake it bread

A quick loaf to serve with a hearty soup of your choice; I love it topped with a slice of cold butter!

- 500 g self-raising flour
- 1 packet mushroom soup powder
- freshly ground black pepper
- 2 cloves garlic, crushed
- 500 ml buttermilk

Preheat the oven to 180 °C. Mix together the flour, mushroom soup powder, pepper and garlic first, then stir through the buttermilk. Spoon into a buttered 1 kg loaf tin dusted with flour, and bake for 55 to 60 minutes, or until a skewer pressed into the middle of the loaf comes out clean.

MAKES 1 LOAF

Bush buns

- 4 cups flour, sifted
- 1 tablespoon salt
- 2 tablespoons sugar
- 10 g instant dry yeast
- 80 g butter, melted
- 1 cup milk
- 1 cup lukewarm water
- 2 eggs, beaten

Mix together the dry ingredients, including the yeast. Mix the butter, milk, water and eggs together and slowly mix into the flour. Turn out onto a lightly floured work surface and knead till the dough is smooth and satiny, and elastic to the touch. If the dough is too wet, knead in a little more flour; too dry, a little more milk.

Place the dough in a lightly oiled bowl and let it rise to twice its size. Knock it down and shape into 24 rolls. Cover and let them rise to twice their size on a flat baking tray.

At this point, once they have risen, you can either open-freeze the rolls on the tray, removing them when they are frozen and storing them in zip lock bags, or bake and eat them straight away.

Place them in a 200 °C oven and bake for 20 to 25 minutes. If you are cooking them on the fire, cook on a nice medium fire, turning occasionally.

MAKES 24 BUNS

TIP: If you are making these in the bush from scratch, let them rise on a foil covered grid that you are going to cook on; otherwise they collapse when you move them. You can also mix up dried milk for these if you don't have any fresh milk available.

Black pepper, Parmesan and anchovy bread sticks

The beauty of these bread sticks is that you can make them up front and open-freeze them. Pack into a sealed container and then bake as many as you need.

- 1 batch of Jenny's basic bread dough
- 4 tablespoons mashed anchovies
- 1 cup sundried tomato pesto
- 1 tablespoon freshly chopped rosemary
- 1 cup grated fresh Parmesan cheese
- 2 tablespoons roughly ground black pepper
- olive oil
- poppy seeds

TIP: Serve with drinks, especially if you are selling the drinks, the anchovy will make them thirsty! Although this is great for fundraising, make sure you can get them home safely.

Preheat the oven to 200 °C. Mix up a batch of Jenny's basic bread dough according to the instructions on page 234. Once the dough has doubled in size, turn out onto a lightly floured surface and cut into two. Roll out each half with a rolling pin till thin and even.

Mix the anchovies with the sundried tomato pesto and rosemary. Divide the pesto into two and spread over the two sheets of dough. Sprinkle over some Parmesan cheese and black pepper.

Fold each sheet of dough over and roll with a rolling pin into a nice, neat rectangle. Cut the dough into 1 cm strips and give them a twist. Place onto a lightly greased baking tray and leave to rise till they double in size. Keep them apart because they will soon be touching each other as the dough expands.

Rest the bread sticks till they have risen a little more, brush lightly with some olive oil, and sprinkle with poppy seeds. Bake for 15 to 20 minutes at 200 °C, or till golden and crisp.

Great alongside tomato soups, or served with a cream cheese and chive dip laced with capers, olives and a little lemon zest.

MAKES LOTS

"Bread deals with living things; with giving life, with growth, with the seed, the grain that nurtures. It is not coincidence that we say bread is the staff of life."

Lionel Poilâne, master baker

CHAPTER FIFTEEN

Sipping

When I was child, we had an enormous mulberry tree in the back garden. It was always so heavy with black, juicy, succulent fruit. The swollen fruit fell to the ground and made a thick carpet under the tree; I loved squishing it under my feet, and I couldn't wear sandals for a week after that.

I can remember the fruit being so huge that my sister Beverley and I had to chew them with our mouths open. The juice would run down our chins onto our clothes and all hell would break loose when we got indoors; my mother would go ballistic about the stains.

My dad used to make mulberry wine and syrup. My mom would wash the berries, sugar them and open-freeze them, and serve them with fresh cream for dessert when they were out of season. I just loved watching that beautiful berry juice bleed into the cream; I would hold the icy fruit in my mouth to warm it, then chew slowly and swallow.

I planted a tree for my son Ryan so that he could enjoy a piece of my childhood. The tree is not nearly like the one I grew up with, but we get to make enough syrup for the year until the next harvest. It is a pity that the birds love them too; they eat the berries and make red poops on the walls of the house, but it's still worth having the tree for the wonderful flavours and memories it offers.

I like to add lots of fresh pomegranate seeds to the glass. I just love to suck the pips clean; they are so swollen with juice and rich in antioxidants!

Pink grapefruit quencher

- 1 cup sugar
- 2 cups gin
- 3 cups fresh grapefruit juice
- ¾ cup fresh lime juice
- ¾ cup Cinzano Bianco
- 1 cup pomegranate seeds
- crushed ice
- chilled soda water to top up the glasses
- extra fresh pomegranate seeds, to garnish
- fresh mint, to garnish

In a large jug, stir the sugar with the gin, grapefruit juice, lime juice and Cinzano Bianco, until dissolved. Stir in the pomegranate seeds. Refrigerate until chilled; about 2 hours.

Fill glasses with crushed ice, top up with grapefruit quencher and soda water, and garnish the glasses with lots of fresh pomegranate seeds and a sprig of fresh mint!

SERVES 8 – 10

Rosemary cocktail

FOR THE SYRUP
- 2 cups warm water
- 1 cup sugar
- 4 large sprigs rosemary

FOR THE COCKTAIL
- slice of orange
- 2 cups freshly squeezed orange juice
- 1 long sprig fresh rosemary
- 1 cup rosemary syrup
- 1 cup of anything white and spirited like vodka, gin, white rum or tequila

To make the syrup, place all the ingredients in a saucepan and simmer till reduced by a third; turn off the heat and let the rosemary infuse while the syrup cools.

Add all the cocktail ingredients to a large jug of crushed ice and top up with sparkling mineral water.

To serve, pour some cocktail mix into tall glasses filled with crushed ice, and top with a sprig of fresh rosemary.

SERVES 4 – 6

"There is a lot more juice in grapefruit than meets the eye."
Author unknown

When I was growing up, we never got things like fizzy drinks, except at Christmas time. Instead my parents would make wine and syrups from all the fruit we grew, which we'd mix with water and drink over ice – lemon, orange, strawberry, mulberry, guava, granadilla. Even prickly pear when they got them, or a special one with apple and cinnamon. We children got the non-alcoholic version of the syrups and my dad got the fruit wines.

Mom would boil the fruit with sugar and water, push it through a sieve to get rid of the pips, then put it back onto the stove to reduce to syrup. She'd strain it into sterilised bottles and jars, which would have simmered in hot water until 'all the germs were dead'.

It never lasted long because we would drink it all as fast as she could make it, and visitors would often leave clutching a bottle or two. No one left our home empty handed.

Mulberry syrup

- 6 cups really ripe mulberries
- 3 cups sugar
- 2 cups water

Soak the dust from the mulberries and put the berries in a saucepan with the sugar and water; simmer with the lid on until the fruit is really soft.

Transfer the fruit and juices to a liquidiser and pulse until the fruit is completely broken down; then strain through a fine sieve and return to the pot and cook till syrupy.

Strain into a clean, sterilised bottle and seal.

MAKES ABOUT 5 CUPS OF SYRUP

TIP: Serve over ice, topped up with vodka and sparkling mineral water. Or drizzle over vanilla ice cream, or into thick natural yoghurt, giving it a swirl to mix it in. Or try it over scones and cream, or with waffles and crumpets.

Cherry brandy

- 500 g morello cherries, washed
- 250 g white sugar
- 600 ml brandy
- 2 star anise
- 1 stick cinnamon
- 3 cloves

This lasts forever – the brandy is divine and the cherries should be eaten a few at a time; they could make you very sleepy!

Sterilise 1 or 2 large preserving jars really well. Prick the cherries and layer them with the sugar in the jars, screw the lid on and leave for 3 days. Give the jars a shake 3 times a day.

After 3 days, place the brandy, star anise, cinnamon and cloves in a saucepan and heat gently. Pour the brandy and spices over the cherries.

Store the jars in a cool, dark place for 3 months. Strain and bottle, or just serve the cherries and brandy over desserts or duck.

MAKES ABOUT 750 ml OF CHERRY BRANDY

Lemon vodka splash

- 2 cups freshly squeezed lemon juice
- 1 cup castor sugar
- 2 cm fresh ginger, peeled and sliced
- vodka, for splashing
- sparkling spring water or soda water

Place the lemon juice, sugar and ginger in a non-stick saucepan and heat gently, stirring until the sugar has dissolved. Bring to the boil, then reduce the heat and simmer until the mixture thickens slightly; remove from the heat and cool.

Fill a tall glass with crushed ice and a few slices of fresh lemon. Add a good slug of vodka, enough lemon syrup to taste, and top up with sparkling spring water or soda.

MAKES ABOUT 2½ CUPS OF SYRUP

TIP: You can leave out the vodka and drizzle the syrup over pancakes, vanilla ice cream or a bowl of fresh berries. Or turn it into a dressing by adding some chopped chillies, some more fresh lemon juice, a little garlic salt and some pepper – not all the syrup silly, just enough to give the dressing a balance! Then, shake it up with a little groundnut oil and splash over a salad.

"Eat when you are hungry, drink when you are dry."
Unknown

Rosy lemon grass syrup

I had the pleasure of climbing a hill in Thailand that was covered with lemon grass. The sun beat down and released the most unbelievable fragrance around me – I love that perfumed grass!

- 1 cup sugar
- 2 cups water
- 6 stems lemon grass
- 5 cm fresh peeled ginger, chopped
- 1 cup frozen mixed berries, pulped
- 1 x 750 ml bottle dry bubbly or sparkling apple juice

Place the sugar and water into a saucepan and start to simmer. Bash the lemon grass so that the entire flavour can be released and add to the pot with the ginger and berries. Simmer for 15 minutes; remove from the heat and cool.

Place the syrup in a blender. Blitz for 30 seconds; strain and chill till you need it.

Pour the syrup into a tall glass and top up with crushed ice and bubbles of your choice. Delicious with a shot of something white and spiritual too!

MAKES ABOUT 3 CUPS OF SYRUP

Fresh lemon fizz

Get your citrus kick this summer. I make jugs of this fresh lemon drink in the summer and never strain it; I love all the zesty bits floating in it! This lemony drink helps to cool things down a bit after you've had a delicious, spicy meal.

- 6 medium ripe lemons, washed
- 1 cup white sugar
- 1 cup water
- crushed ice
- soda water or sparkling mineral water
- fresh mint, for garnishing
- sliced lemon, for garnishing

Cut the lemon into eighths with the skin on, pips removed. Place the lemon and sugar into the bowl of your processor and blitz till fine; add the water and blitz again.

Scoop the lemon syrup into a large jug. Fill a tall glass with crushed ice and add a third of a cup of syrup. Top with the fizzy water of your choice, and garnish with fresh mint and lemon slices.

MAKES ABOUT 4 CUPS OF SYRUP

TIP: This is yummy and quenching with tonic water, and yes, you can add a slug of your favourite gin to it for an amazing lift!

I keep the lemon syrup in the freezer in ice cube trays for a quick fix on a hot summer's day.

"We are living in a
world today where
lemonade is made from
artificial flavours and
furniture polish is made
from real lemons."
Alfred E. Newman

CHAPTER SIXTEEN

Sweet Talk

My Granny Cannon was famous for her steamed sponge. The fragrance from that hot, sticky pudding would entice me into her kitchen without fail; I make it to this day for my own family.

My granny really knew how to tempt my sweet tooth. How I loved it when she made a sweet sandwich after lunch with two Nestlé penny chocolates. I would get all excited when she took them out of the kitchen cupboard; I can still see those red wrappers in her knobbly hands.

She would cut a thick slice of white bread, remove the crusts, slit a pocket into it and stuff it with sliced banana and the two penny chocolates. She would beat up a few eggs with honey and vanilla essence and then soak the bread in it for just long enough to absorb the egg. When the butter hissed and bubbled in a frying pan, she would cook the bread till it was golden and crisp, slice it open and drizzle with more honey – my first ever French toast!

Jenny's celebration tiramisu

This yummy tiramisu works like a dream for a festive celebration when you want to serve a dessert that looks and tastes special. I make it in a round cake tin and decorate the top with chopped preserved figs, cherries, chopped chocolate and a light dusting of cocoa powder.

- 2 cups strong, black coffee
- ½ cup dark rum, or more if you are brave
- 4 eggs, separated
- ¼ cup castor sugar
- 500 g mascarpone cheese
- 1 cup cream, whipped
- 1 large vanilla sponge cake, cut into fingers
- 1 cup glacé cherries, halved
- 1 cup chopped toasted almonds
- 1 cup chopped preserved figs
- some chopped chocolate
- 2 teaspoons dark cocoa powder

"Seize the moment. Remember all those women on the Titanic who waved off the dessert cart."
Erma Bombeck

Mix together the coffee and the rum. Set aside to cool.

Using an electric beater, beat the egg yolks and sugar for about 3 minutes until the mixture is thick and pale. Now add the mascarpone and beat until just combined. Using a metal spoon, fold in the whipped cream.

Beat the egg whites until they form soft peaks. Fold quickly and lightly into the cream mixture with a metal spoon.

Now dip half the cake fingers, one at a time of course, into the rum and coffee mixture. Drain off any excess liquid and arrange the cake fingers in the base of your serving dish (about 20 cm x 25 cm and 6 cm deep). You can use a round springform cake tin, if you prefer. Spread half the cream mixture over the dipped cake fingers.

Mix the fruit and nuts together and spread half the mixture over the cream-covered cake.

Now it's time to dip the remaining cake fingers in the coffee, and repeat layering with the cake fingers and cream mixture. Even out the top and dust with cocoa powder. To make serving easier, dust the cocoa in lines, dividing the tiramisu into equal portions.

Place the rest of the nut and fruit mixture in little piles on top of the tiramisu, either in the middle or in the cocoa-lined squares. Sprinkle over some chopped chocolate, if you like. Place the tiramisu in the fridge for at least 4 hours to allow the flavours to get to know each other and for the dessert to set.

To serve, cut slices with a wet knife on the cocoa lines between the fruit and nut piles, and place on a plate. Dust with some icing sugar, and maybe a bit more cocoa.

SERVES 8

TIP: You can use boudoir biscuits instead of sponge cake, if you prefer.

I can't imagine my life without a fig in it. This sexy, sweet, juicy-fleshed, biblical fruit, full of crunchy seeds, transports me to paradise. Even the thought of a wasp making her home inside the body of the fig for a short while doesn't turn me off, unlike some people I know.

When figs are really ripe, the juice oozes out of them and that is the way it should be. I am lucky to own two fig trees and I have to fight with the birds to keep the fruit on the tree for as long as possible so that they can ripen.

Figs have stacks of potassium and they contain impressive amounts of fibre, so let your body make full use of them when they are in season!

Figgy panettone bread and butter pudding

The wonderful thing about a fig is that it freezes so well; when my fig trees are swollen with more fresh fruit than I know what to do with, I always open-freeze a few kilos. Then I can make this delicious pudding long after the season is over.

- 10 ripe figs, sliced lengthways into quarters
- 125 ml honey
- ¾ cup dried cranberries
- 1 medium panettone, cut into 5 thick slices
- 2 whole eggs
- 2 extra egg yolks
- grated zest of 1 orange
- 30 ml castor sugar
- 500 ml cream
- ½ teaspoon ground cinnamon
- sugar, for sprinkling

Butter a 1.5 litre oven-proof dish. Place half the sliced figs on the bottom of the dish, drizzle with honey, and scatter on the cranberries.

Cut each slice of panettone into 4 triangles and pack them onto the sliced figs. Mix together the eggs, extra egg yolks, orange zest, sugar, cream and cinnamon, and pour over the panettone. Leave to stand, covered, for 30 minutes.

Preheat the oven to 180 °C. Arrange the remaining sliced figs over the pudding, sprinkle with a little sugar and bake for 40 to 50 minutes, until crisp and lightly browned on top.

Serve warm, or even deliciously cold the next day!

SERVES 6

TIP: If you don't have panettone, you can use 5 thick slices of raisin bread instead.

"Life is uncertain.
Eat dessert first."
Ernestine Ulmer

Top me with anything cheesecake

I love a wedge of baked cheesecake with a strong cup of tea, but cheesecake also makes a wonderful dessert; you can top it with whatever makes your mouth happy.

THE CRUST

- ½ packet ginger biscuits
- ½ packet tennis biscuits
- 100 g toasted almonds
- 100 g soft butter, cubed

THE FILLING

- 600 g cream cheese
- 60 g castor sugar
- 1 tablespoon flour
- 150 ml runny honey
- 4 large eggs
- 2 teaspoons lemon juice
- zest of 1 lemon or orange

Make the crust first. Place the biscuits and nuts into the bowl of a food processor and whizz it all up to resemble fine crumbs. Now add the butter and whizz till it all comes together.

Press the mixture into a 20 cm springform cake tin. Smooth it off and then pop it into the fridge to chill out and firm up; about 30 minutes.

Preheat the oven to 170 °C. Now make the filling. Mix together the cream cheese, sugar, flour and honey. Beat in the eggs, one at a time, till well incorporated and smooth, then add the lemon juice and zest and stir in well. (If you want to do this in a machine, feel free to do it without guilt – more time for a bubble bath!)

Spoon the filling into the cake tin; you know, the one in the fridge! Now that the tin is filled and smoothed down, pop it into the oven and bake it for about 1 hour and 15 minutes. Check on it after 60 minutes – the middle should jiggle a bit, but if it is very wobbly let it bake a little longer.

Turn the oven off and let the cheesecake set in the oven till it cools down. Remove from the oven and let the cheesecake cool down completely. Cover well and chill in the fridge till needed.

Remove the cake from the fridge and bring it to room temperature before removing from the cake tin; we don't want any accidents now, do we?

It's time to top me! This cheesecake is delicious with so many different toppings. Do try chocolate ganache and fresh raspberries; caramelised oranges; honey and nuts; mascarpone with tons of fresh berries; or fresh figs and mascarpone with honey and toasted almonds.

SERVES 6 – 8

> "Strawberries are the angels of the earth; innocent and sweet with green leafy wings reaching heavenward."
> *Terri Guillemets*

Strawberries in port syrup

We are into boozy berries in my house and port just works beautifully with strawberries. This freezes like a dream and when the season is over, I warm it up and serve it hot over ice cream or rice pudding in the winter.

- ¾ cup ruby port
- 3 tablespoons castor sugar
- 2 cloves
- thin peel of 1 orange, all pith removed
- 1 kg ripe medium-sized strawberries

Place the port, sugar, cloves and orange peel in a small saucepan and simmer gently till the castor sugar has dissolved; about 5 minutes. Set aside to cool.

Hull and slice the strawberries thickly and pour over the port. Stir to coat and let the strawberries rest in the fridge till you are ready to serve them. Spoon the strawberries over big blobs of vanilla ice cream.

SERVES 4–6

Watermelon granita

Watermelon has a beautiful fresh clean flavour, but sometimes I get one that does not live up to its expectation, so instead of flinging it into the compost I make a batch of granita!

- 450 g deseeded watermelon, roughly chopped into small pieces
- 1 tablespoon castor sugar
- ½–1 teaspoon fresh lemon juice
- ⅓ cup water

Place the watermelon in a blender and blitz it up finely.

Place the castor sugar, lemon juice and water in a saucepan and heat while stirring to dissolve the sugar. Add the watermelon and give it a good mix. Pour into a plastic dish, cover and freeze.

Take a fork and break up the ice crystals every half an hour. When you are ready to serve the granita, run a fork through the crystals, spoon into pretty glasses and serve.

SERVES 4

"Stressed spelled backwards is desserts. Coincidence? I think not!" *Author unknown*

Jenny's carrot cake

This delicious cake of mine is especially for Abdul Isaacs, who bakes it a minimum of three times a month for my family!

THE CAKE
- 2 cups cake flour
- 1 teaspoon salt
- 2 teaspoons baking powder
- 1½ teaspoons bicarbonate of soda
- 2½ teaspoons ground cinnamon
- 2 cups sugar
- 1½ cups sunflower oil
- 4 eggs, beaten
- 2 cups finely grated carrot
- 1 cup canned crushed pineapple, lightly drained
- 1 cup toasted finely chopped walnuts or pecan nuts
- 1 cup desiccated coconut
- ½ cup poppy seeds

THE ICING
- 200 g butter
- 400 g icing sugar
- 250 g cream cheese, chilled
- 1 teaspoon vanilla extract

Preheat the oven to 180 °C. Combine the first 5 ingredients in a large bowl. Then stir in the sugar, oil and eggs, and mix well. Thoroughly blend in the carrot, pineapple, walnuts, coconut and poppy seeds.

Turn the batter out into a greased and floured 24 to 26 cm springform baking tin. Bake for 65 to 70 minutes, or until firm and risen and pulling away from the sides of the tin. Cool briefly in the tin, and then turn out onto a wire rack to cool completely before icing.

To make the icing, first beat the butter until softened, then stir in the icing sugar till well blended. Carefully stir in the chilled cream cheese and vanilla extract, do not over-stir as you will make the icing separate.

Ice the cake and serve.

SERVES 10

I have a beautiful peach tree in my garden that offers my family the gift of the most luscious, fragrant, juicy fruit that there is to be had. Even after sharing them, there are so many left and, besides eating them fresh, they get bottled by my mother, and baked and turned into jam by me.

Oh my goodness! The sun is beating down on my peach tree which is just below my bedroom patio and the scent of peaches is just so overwhelming. Oh, why can't I bottle it? What an aroma; it makes me dizzy!

Baked peaches with ricotta and almonds

This dessert captures the fragrance of summer for me!

- 120 g ricotta cheese
- 60 g ground almonds
- 30 ml Amaretto liqueur
- 2 egg whites
- 115 g castor sugar
- 4 large peaches, halved and stoned
- 30 g flaked almonds
- 3 tablespoons honey
- 3 tablespoons whiskey

Preheat the oven to 200 °C. Mix the ricotta, ground almonds and liqueur together in a mixing bowl. In a scrupulously clean glass bowl, whisk the egg whites to soft peaks, slowly adding the castor sugar till the mixture is nice and stiff. Fold the meringue gently into the ricotta.

Place the peaches in a single layer in an oven-proof dish. Spoon the ricotta and almond mixture onto the peaches, top with flaked almonds and bake for 15 to 20 minutes so that the peaches are tender and the topping puffed up and golden.

Heat the honey and whiskey together until the honey foams, then cool and drizzle over the peaches. Serve with vanilla ice cream or a scoop of mascarpone. Delicious served hot or cold!

SERVES 4

> "I feel a recipe is only a theme, which an intelligent cook can play each time with a variation."
> *Madame Benoit*

Orange and honey semolina cake

Semolina is really very versatile; you can use it to make sweet and savoury dishes. In our home we use it as a porridge, or to make gnocchi and bake cakes.

FOR THE SYRUP
- ¾ cup runny honey
- juice of 2 oranges

THE CAKE
- zest of 2 oranges
- 200 g semolina
- 100 g brown sugar
- 100 g cake flour
- 30 g ground almonds
- 1 teaspoon baking powder
- 50 g salted butter, melted
- 150 ml buttermilk
- 20 whole blanched toasted almonds, for garnishing

Place the ingredients for the syrup in a small saucepan and boil till reduced by a quarter of the volume. Set aside to cool.

Preheat the oven to 180 °C. Place the orange zest, semolina, sugar, flour, ground almonds and baking powder in a large mixing bowl. Mix well to incorporate all the ingredients.

Make a well in the centre of the dry ingredients and add the butter and buttermilk. Mix together to incorporate the dry ingredients – the dough will be quite stiff. Spoon into a well-greased square baking tin, smooth the surface and bake for 25 to 30 minutes.

Remove from the oven and decorate the top with the almonds. Pour over the syrup and return to the oven for a further 10 minutes. Cool and cut!

SERVES 6

This is such a traditional dessert; really delicious and well worth making. It is dedicated to my beautiful boy, Henri Slier, who could not get enough of this pudding when we were filming together in Thailand. I got it wrong initially because I was boiling the rice instead of steaming it, and Henri was disappointed. Although it tasted good, making it with steamed rice is so much better. I love to serve it with delicious, juicy, fragrant slices of ripe mango!

Sticky rice pudding for Henri

When we were young I loved to stir my mother's homemade mulberry jam into rice pudding or just drizzle it with homemade mulberry syrup.

- ⅔ cup glutinous white rice
- 1 cup coconut milk, plus extra for drizzling
- 3 tablespoons sugar
- pinch of salt
- 2 ripe, firm mangoes, peeled and cubed or sliced, then chilled

Soak and rinse the rice several times; then soak it overnight in fresh water.

The next day, drain the rice. Line a steamer with a piece of muslin cloth or a very clean tea towel, spread the rice evenly over the cloth, and cover the basket. Steam over a pot of simmering water for around 20 to 25 minutes, or until the rice is nice and tender.

Now place the coconut milk in a saucepan, add the sugar and salt and warm gently, stirring all the time until the sugar has dissolved. Bring to the boil, then remove the saucepan from the heat and cool the coconut milk.

Place the rice in a bowl and stir the coconut milk into it. Mix it together well and let it stand for 20 minutes.

Spoon the rice onto serving plates, top with mangoes and drizzle with some coconut milk.

Cherries, litchis and preserved ginger also work well with this pudding. I love to spoon coconut milk and palm sugar syrup over the rice as well, but you can decide how you would like to eat it, Henri!

SERVES 4

TIP: If you are in a hurry to make your pudding, soak the rice for 1 hour in hot water before steaming it.

Dark chocolate is wonderfully indulgent. I love it for its full, delicious flavour and for the fact that only two people in my house eat it! The others find it difficult not to eat the whole slab of milk chocolate if they come across it, so the only way to keep chocolate in my house is to ensure that it is dark and dense. Or so I thought; the whole family has now discovered the joys of 80 per cent chocolate melted into hot milk with a drizzle of honey!

Chocolate makes you feel good; it is said that it stimulates the secretion of endorphins, producing pleasurable sensations. It also contains serotonin, a neurotransmitter that is said to act as an anti-depressant. So, no guilt!

Chocolate orange ricotta tart

THE CRUST
- 120 g cake flour
- 100 g ground almonds
- 100 g chilled unsalted butter, cubed
- zest of 1 orange
- 50 g castor sugar
- yolk of 1 egg
- 1–2 tablespoons orange juice

THE FILLING
- 250 g ricotta cheese
- 250 ml fresh cream, lightly beaten
- 2 tablespoons castor sugar
- 1 tablespoon honey
- 1 tablespoon fresh orange zest
- 2 eggs, beaten
- juice of 1 orange
- 200 g dark chocolate, roughly chopped

Make the crust first. Fling the flour, almonds, butter, orange zest and castor sugar into your food processor and blitz till it resembles breadcrumbs; take care not to over-process it! Now add the egg yolk and enough orange juice to just bring it together; you should have a firm dough.

Remove and knead lightly on a lightly floured surface, and chill briefly. Roll the dough out to line a 23 cm loose-bottomed flan tin and chill for 20 minutes.

Meanwhile, mix all the filling ingredients together and keep aside.

Preheat the oven to 180 °C. I like to bake the base blind so that I don't have a soggy-bottomed tart. Line the pastry base with greaseproof paper and top with dried beans. Bake for 12 minutes at 180 °C, remove the beans and fill the pastry base with the filling.

Bake for 25 minutes, or until a skewer comes out clean. Dust with icing sugar, top with chocolate curls and serve.

SERVES 6

"Chocolate is the answer.
Who cares what the question is?"
Author unknown

Berry meringue slice

THE MERINGUE

- 4 fresh egg whites
- 1 cup castor sugar
- ½ teaspoon vanilla extract
- 1 teaspoon white vinegar

THE TOPPING

- 2 teaspoons castor sugar
- 500 g mixed berries
- ⅓ cup strawberry or youngberry jam
- 2 teaspoons brandy
- 1 teaspoon ground caraway seeds
- 1½ cups chilled whipped cream, or mascarpone

This is a delicious dessert, tangy with fresh berries, and creamy and sweet with ground caraway seeds.

Preheat the oven to 150 °C and make the meringue base. Beat the egg whites in a scrupulously clean glass bowl until soft peaks form. Now gradually add the sugar, beating well after each addition, until all the sugar has dissolved. Mix the vanilla and vinegar together, add it to the egg white and beat for 1 minute.

Line an oven tray with baking paper and dust lightly with cornflour. Now spread the meringue carefully onto the tray. Bake for 45 minutes on the middle shelf of the oven until the shell feels crisp and hard. Be very careful now; lift the meringue onto a wire rack to cool down.

Make the topping while you wait. Sprinkle the sugar over the berries and chill. Warm the jam, brandy and caraway seeds together, strain and get ready to assemble the slice.

Just before serving, spoon the cream onto the meringue, top with the chilled berries, and spoon over the jam.

SERVES 4–6

TIP: Instead of using mixed berries, you could use just one type of berry if you prefer.

We go to Klondyke Cherry Farm in Ceres once a year to pick fresh cherries; we dip them in chocolate, make jam, juice them for syrups and freeze them for later in the year to make this yummy pudding!

Chocolate cherry pie

THE CRUST
- 70 g melted butter
- 250 g chocolate coated biscuits, crumbed
- a good pinch of ground ginger

THE FILLING
- 100 g good-quality dark chocolate, chopped
- 50 g unsalted butter
- 50 ml runny honey
- ⅔ cup brown sugar
- 3 eggs, beaten
- 2 tablespoons brandy
- 1 cup tinned sour cherries, or stewed fresh cherries

Make the crust first. Mix together the butter, crumbs and ground ginger, and press down well into the base of a 23 cm loose-bottomed cake tin. Now chill till firm. Make the filling while the base chills.

Preheat the oven to 180 °C. Place a glass bowl over a pot of gently simmering water and add the chocolate, butter and honey. Melt together slowly. Remove from the heat and stir in the sugar, eggs and brandy.

Remove the base from the fridge, spread the cherries onto the bottom (if using tinned cherries, be sure to drain them well first!) and pour the filling over the top.

Place the pie in the preheated oven and bake for 35 to 40 minutes, or until set. Remove from the oven and cool.

Serve with lashings of whipped cream or scoops of mascarpone cheese.

SERVES 4 – 6

> "Strength is the capacity to break a chocolate bar into four pieces with your bare hands – and then eat just one of the pieces."
> *Judith Viorst*

Fresh figgy chocolate tart

THE PASTRY
- 100 g flour
- 500 g ground almonds
- 30 g cocoa
- 800 g chilled butter, cubed
- 4 tablespoons castor sugar
- 4 egg yolks

THE FILLING
- 1½ tubs mascarpone cheese
- 1 cup toasted and chopped walnuts
- honey for drizzling
- 200 g dark chocolate, melted
- 8 ripe, swollen fresh figs
- 1 tablespoon rose or orange blossom water (optional)

Put the flour, almonds, cocoa, butter and sugar into a food processor and whizz till it resembles fine breadcrumbs. (Or you could make the pastry by hand, making sure your hands are really cold and working the ingredients very lightly till you achieve the breadcrumbs – up to you!) Add the egg yolks and, if needed, about a tablespoon of cold water.

Whizz till it comes together in a smooth, firm dough. Wrap it in plastic and keep in the fridge for about 50 minutes.

Now that the pastry has had a chance to chill out, grease a 20 cm loose-based tart tin and roll it out between 2 sheets of greaseproof paper. Press the pastry into the tin, in all the nooks and crannies.

Roll the rolling pin over the top of the tart tin to trim off the rough bits, cover the bottom with greaseproof paper and fill with dried beans. Bake in a preheated oven at 180 °C for about 12 minutes. Remove the paper and beans, then bake for another 10 minutes or until crisp and golden. Allow to cool completely.

Now you are ready to fill the shell. Spread the mascarpone onto the base of the tart and cover with half the chopped nuts and a little honey. Drizzle with the melted chocolate.

Quarter the figs, sprinkle with rosewater if you are using it, and then arrange them over the top of the tart. Drizzle liberally with honey and sprinkle over the remaining nuts.

SERVES 6

TIP: I use dried soya beans to line my pastry shells when I blind bake them.

Iced berry terrine

THE TERRINE
- 1 large Madeira sponge cake, or panettone
- 300 g each ripe strawberries, blueberries and raspberries
- 2 litres vanilla ice cream, slightly softened

THE TOPPING
- 250 g frozen raspberries
- 200 g fresh or frozen blueberries
- 200 g sliced strawberries
- 1 tablespoon icing sugar

Line a 900 g loaf tin with cling film, making sure it overlaps the sides of the tin so that you can fold it over the dessert.

Place a layer of vanilla ice cream onto the base of the tin, and on top of that place a few thin slices of sponge cake. Cover with a row of strawberries, next to that a row of blueberries, and next to that a row of raspberries.

Cover the berries with vanilla ice cream, and continue layering as before till the loaf tin is full. Press down firmly to make sure you seal all the holes. Fold the cling film over the top. Place the tin in the freezer and freeze till really hard.

Remove the terrine from the freezer 15 minutes before you want to serve it. Dip quickly in warm water, and unmould it onto a platter. Top with the berries, and give it a good shake of icing sugar.

YIELDS 8 – 10 SLICES

TIP: For easier slicing, dip your knife in hot water.

"Ice cream is exquisite.
What a pity it isn't illegal."
Voltaire

H ere is my Granny Cannon's famous steamed sponge – try it, you'll love it! I like to add a few delicious bits to the bottom of the bowl to ring the changes.

Granny Cannon's steamed sponge

- 6 tablespoons honey, or golden syrup
- 125 g butter
- 70 g castor sugar
- 2 beaten eggs
- 1 ½ cups cake flour, sifted
- 1 ½ teaspoons baking powder
- 3 tablespoons milk

Spoon the honey or syrup into the base of a buttered 1 litre heat-proof pudding bowl. Cream together the butter and sugar until light and fluffy, and then beat the eggs in one at a time.

Mix the flour and baking powder together and fold it into the butter mix with the milk. Spoon the mixture into your pudding bowl, cover with foil and tie securely with string.

Place an inverted saucer onto the base of a saucepan big enough to hold the bowl. Put the pudding bowl onto the saucer, pour boiling water into the saucepan to reach two-thirds of the way up the bowl, cover and cook for 2 hours. Keep topping up with boiling water as the level drops.

When the pudding is done, invert onto a shallow dish. Serve with dollops of mascarpone cheese or vanilla ice cream, thick Greek yoghurt and toasted pecans, or even a sticky caramel sauce. I love serving red berries on the side with sweet, rosewater-scented whipped cream or mascarpone – try it!

SERVES 4

VARIATIONS: I sometimes like to add a few delicious things to the bottom of the bowl before pouring in the pudding batter. Instead of syrup, try some honey, figs and walnuts. Or, if you like, you could scatter a few tablespoons of chopped ginger on the base of the bowl, or even a cup of youngberry or apricot jam to give this dessert a fruity spin.

Mulberry sponge

When the mulberry tree is so heavy with fruit it can't stay on the branches, I harvest them from under the tree because they are firm, fabulously juicy and sweet. I give them a good soak to get rid of the dust and then decide how to use them – in tarts, syrup or jam, or under a spongy layer of almonds drenched with honey.

- 100 g unsalted butter
- 100 g sugar
- 2 jumbo eggs
- 2 tablespoons whiskey
- zest of 1 orange
- ½ cup self-raising flour
- 100 g ground almonds
- 500 g cleaned, ripe mulberries
- juice of 1 orange
- honey, for drizzling
- 30 g butter, for dotting

Preheat the oven to 180 °C. Cream the butter and sugar together till pale, light and nice and fluffy. Now beat in the eggs, one at a time. Stir in the whiskey and zest, sift the flour over the surface of the mixture and fold in, then fold in the ground almonds.

Place the mulberries into a greased baking dish, stir in the orange juice and spoon the batter mixture over the berries. Drizzle with honey, dot with butter and bake at 180 °C for about 40 minutes. Check the centre with a skewer; if it comes out clean and dry remove the sponge from the oven, otherwise let it bake for a few more minutes.

Serve with scoops of vanilla ice cream, or great dollops of mascarpone cheese, or whipped cream, or even thick lovely Greek yoghurt.

SERVES 4

TIP: If you can't get mulberries, you can use blackberries or youngberries instead.

It made my heart glad to see Marga stuff more mulberries into her mouth than we picked this season. Every home should have a mulberry tree!

Coffee and pecan creams with whiskey syrup

COFFEE CREAMS
- 4 ¼ teaspoons powdered gelatine
- 1 cup milk
- 2 teaspoons really good instant coffee dissolved in a little water
- ⅔ cup castor sugar
- 6 egg yolks
- 150 g toasted pecan nuts, finely ground
- 1 ½ cups whipping cream
- chopped nuts, for sprinkling

WHISKEY SYRUP
- ½ cup honey
- 2 tablespoons whiskey

First things first – let's dissolve the gelatine by adding about 1 ½ tablespoons of cold water to the powder in a glass bowl. Place the bowl over a double boiler and stir till the gelatine has dissolved; set aside. Then heat the milk and coffee in a small saucepan; don't boil it!

Now get a bowl going over a pot of simmering water; don't let the bottom touch. Place the sugar and egg yolks into the bowl and whisk away until the mixture is pale. Gradually add in the milk, whisking all the time. Continue stirring till the mixture thickens. Remove from the heat and slowly stir in the gelatine and the nuts. Let the mixture cool and then chill it until almost set.

Have your moulds ready to fill; grease them lightly. Whip the cream to the soft peak stage and fold it into the jelly mix. Spoon into the moulds and set in the fridge.

Just before you are ready to serve, make the whiskey syrup. Heat together the honey and whiskey till the honey foams. Remove from the heat and cool.

Unmould the coffee creams, drizzle with whiskey syrup and sprinkle with chopped nuts.

SERVES 4

Cheat's coffee ice cream

My family would eat ice cream for breakfast, if I let them! When they feel like a bowl of ice cream and the freezer is bare, I whip up a quick batch of this delicious treat without having to start from scratch by making a fresh egg custard.

- 1 litre Ultra Mel vanilla custard
- 397 g tin condensed milk
- 4 tablespoons strong instant coffee granules
- 1 cup milk

Whisk the custard and condensed milk together, and then dissolve the coffee granules in the milk. Now whisk the milk into the custard and chill for an hour. Pour into your ice cream machine and start churning.

If you don't have an ice cream machine, pour into a freezer-proof container and freeze. Once the ice cream has frozen, remove from the freezer and, using an electric beater, beat it well to break up the crystals. Return to the freezer and repeat the process once more; this will give you a nice smooth ice cream.

SERVES 4 – 6

TIP: I stir a cup of chopped almonds into the ice cream before I serve it!

CHAPTER SEVENTEEN

Getting *Pickled*

My mother is the jam queen. If it is abundant, sweet, fresh and fruity, she makes jam. She has words with the birds if they don't leave her enough fruit on her trees for jam-making!

During the pineapple harvesting season in Natal, the farmers would load up their trucks with fragrantly ripe pineapples and drive from Hluhluwe to sell their crop to the city dwellers. I used to love the smell of the ripe fruit and would stand at the truck for hours banking the aroma for later. My mother would buy so many pineapples on a Sunday afternoon and would spend the whole week chopping, peeling, juicing and preserving.

Even though my mom wasn't a very good dessert maker, you could still smell the buttery fragrance of her pastries wafting through the house; amazing apple pies and jam tarts. When mulberries were in season she'd make this beautiful, hunky, chunky jam for the tarts. My god, I loved it! She always thought she'd make enough jam to last until the next season, but of course it never did.

My mother is 84 now and just this last season, from the trees in my garden, she made quite a few jars of her gorgeous mulberry jam. I just love it, love it, love it!

My beautiful lemon tree is 24 years old and it took 10 years to get her to where she is now. The many conversations and trunk-rubbing sessions have ensured that she is always either in fruit, flower or bud – she just keeps giving. Oh, I just love her!

I never pick a lemon from my tree unless it is well and truly ripe.

Spicy preserved lemons

- 8 washed, unwaxed, ripe lemons
- 8 tablespoons coarse sea salt
- 1 tablespoon black peppercorns
- 1 teaspoon toasted cumin seeds
- 4 green cardamom pods, split
- 1 teaspoon coriander seeds, toasted
- 4 dried bird's eye chillies
- 6 unpeeled garlic cloves, bashed to release the flavour
- 2 fresh bay leaves
- olive oil

Cut the lemons into quarters lengthways. Layer the lemons and salt in a sieve to drain over a glass bowl for 48 hours.

Place the salty lemon wedges with all the spices, chillies, garlic and bay leaves into a large, well-sterilised glass jar with a tight-fitting lid.

Cover the lemons with olive oil, seal the jar and store for 9 weeks in a cool, dark place.

Preserved lemons feature in Moroccan cooking, but there are so many ways to use them. I love them in salad dressings, rice dishes, fish cakes, and even chopped into lamb burger mix. Play around a bit; I do!

"Hunger is the best pickle."
Benjamin Franklin

When you are a child and something comes in a bottle, you are amazed when you see your parents make the same thing at home. Saturday mornings really early, off to the Indian market in Warrick Avenue in Durban with my mother Thelma to buy the vegetables for the weekend, and for making piccalilli.

I loved my mother's piccalilli because it was so crunchy and tart and addictive, and the mustard seeds burst and popped in your mouth!

My piccalilli

When you make piccalilli, you have to make sure that there is not one blemish on the vegetables; they have to be really fresh.

- 1 beautiful, big, snowy white cauliflower
- 400 g English cucumber, cut lengthways
- 300 g young, really fresh green beans
- 500 g baby onions
- 300 g carrots, peeled
- 1 cup salt
- 10 cups water
- 1 cup white sugar
- 2 teaspoons white mustard seeds
- 2 teaspoons English mustard powder
- 4 cups white wine vinegar
- 1 heaped tablespoon ground turmeric
- 2 tablespoons fresh ginger, peeled and finely chopped
- 2 large green chillies, split down the middle lengthways
- 6 large cloves garlic, peeled and sliced
- ¼ cup flour

Break the cauliflower into florets with the stems. Cut the cucumber lengthways and, using a spoon, scrape out the seeds. Cut the cucumber into rough chunks. Top and tail the beans and slice each into 3 pieces. Peel and quarter the baby onions, and chop the carrots roughly.

Layer the vegetables in a large glass bowl, sprinkling the salt on each layer. Pour the water over the vegetables and cover with cling film. Soak for 24 hours.

Drain the vegetables after 24 hours and rinse them thoroughly, a few times, and then dry well.

Place the sugar, mustard seeds, mustard powder, vinegar and turmeric in a large stainless steel saucepan. Add the ginger, chilli and garlic, and cook gently until the sugar has dissolved. Add the vegetables and bring to the boil, and then simmer for about 10 minutes. Do not over-cook!

Mix the flour with some of the pot juices to make a thin paste. Stir into the vegetables and cook for a few minutes till it thickens.

Spoon into hot sterilised jars, store in a dark place for 2 weeks, and use within 6 months. Store in the fridge once the jar has been opened.

This piccalilli is great on cheese sarmies, or served with cold meats such as ham and corned beef.

MAKES ABOUT 2 kg

TIP: Never eat directly from the bottle, as the saliva left on the spoon will contaminate the contents and you will have no more!

Lemon and thyme marinated olives

When choosing your oil for this recipe, I would highly recommend the gorgeous lemon infused olive oil from Willow Creek. Their range of award–winning extra virgin olive oils is made on their family farm in the Nuy Valley.

- 1 kg large, firm green olives, with pips
- ½ cup snipped fresh thyme sprigs, bashed
- 6 cloves peeled garlic, thickly sliced
- 1 perfect fresh bay leaf, thinly sliced
- ½ teaspoon cumin seeds, toasted and bashed
- ½ teaspoon coriander seeds, toasted and bashed
- ½ teaspoon toasted fennel seeds, bashed
- 2 dried red chillies, roughly chopped
- peel of 2 unwaxed lemons, thinly sliced and chopped
- extra virgin olive oil
- lemon infused olive oil

Sterilise a glass bottle large enough to hold the olives. Make sure that it has a tight-fitting lid.

Cut a slit into each olive going all the way through to the pip. Mix the rest of the ingredients, except the olive oil, into the olives and stir well. Pack the olives with all the herbs and spices into the sterilised jar and top up with enough olive oil to cover them – I like to use half olive oil and half lemon infused olive oil. Seal tightly and store in a cool dark place for two weeks.

Spoon the olives with a little of the infused oil over salads or serve them with drinks. The oil is delicious spooned over boiled potatoes and savoury rice, or used in salad dressings.

TIP: I always bash the thyme and spices so that the flavours can be released more easily.

Beetroot relish

This is delicious on cheese, cooked meats, steamed fish and sandwiches.

- 4 tablespoons olive oil
- ½ kg sweet red onions, peeled and sliced
- 3 cloves fresh garlic, crushed
- 2 red chillies, sliced
- 1 star anise
- ½ tablespoon black peppercorns
- 2 cloves
- 1 kg small sweet beetroots, peeled and coarsely grated
- 150 ml good-quality white wine vinegar
- 325 g brown sugar
- salt, to taste

Heat the olive oil and very slowly cook down the onions and garlic with the chillies, star anise, peppercorns and cloves. Keep stirring for about 5 minutes, and do not burn!

Add the beetroot and cook for 5 minutes, then add the vinegar and sugar, and cook for a further 20 minutes. Season with salt and remove from the heat.

Cool and bottle in sterilised glass jars and store in the refrigerator.

MAKES ABOUT 4 LARGE JARS

TIP: Get your partner to grate the beetroot for you!

Pickled turnips

I can't imagine a falafel without pickled turnips, grilled aubergines, chillies or hummus. Actually, I just love turnips in any shape or form; sadly they are such an underrated vegetable.

- 1.2 kg young turnips, well washed
- 3 beetroots, well washed
- 3 tablespoons coarse salt
- 6 cups water
- juice of 2 lemons
- 1 teaspoon coriander seeds, roasted
- 4 cloves unpeeled garlic, bashed
- peel of 2 lemons, thinly sliced, without the pith
- 4 green chillies, roughly sliced

Cut the unpeeled, raw turnips and beetroots into slices.

Place the salt and water in a glass bowl and stir until the salt has dissolved.

Divide the beetroot between 4 large sterilised glass jars and pour in the lemon juice. Top with turnips, coriander seeds, garlic, lemon peel and chillies, and cover with the brine. Make sure that you cover everything completely with the brine.

Seal the jars and store in a cool, dark place.

MAKES ABOUT 4 LARGE JARS

THE GOOD NEWS: You can use this pickle after a week and a half – all pink, crunchy and spicy!

I am lucky to know someone with lots of pomegranate trees who kindly lets me share the harvest each year.

I am sure it was not an apple but a pomegranate, the seeded apple, that tempted Eve in the Garden of Eden; how could anyone resist those beautiful ruby seeds so swollen with juice?

The pomegranate has been used in folk medicine for centuries in the Middle East, India and Iran. It has fantastic antioxidant properties and contains substantial amounts of potassium, fibre, vitamin C and niacin; but you will only get those benefits if you suck the flesh off those beautiful seeds.

All those plump seeds housed in one fruit tell me it has to be a symbol of fertility – I think they should have been called 'passion fruit'!

My pomegranate molasses

- 18 large pomegranates
- ¾ cup brown sugar
- ½ cup freshly squeezed lemon juice

To juice the fruit, crack open the pomegranates, and peel away the white protective layers to remove the seeds. What really works well is a good smack on the bottom with a heavy object to loosen them from the shell.

Give your hands a good wash and place the seeds in a sieve over a clean bowl. Now rub the seeds gently up and down over the sieve until they have given you all of their juices (maybe you should wear rubber gloves for this). Don't go rubbing like crazy because as you get closer to the pip, it is bitter and so is the pith.

Strain the juice into a saucepan, throw the seeds onto the compost heap (or dry them and use in curries), and add the sugar and lemon juice. Stir the juices and sugar together and then simmer to reduce the liquid to one cup. Bottle in a clean sterilised jar.

This molasses can be used as a base for dressings and sauces.

MAKES 1 CUP

TIP: Choose pomegranates that feel heavy for their size – the seeds will be plump and full of juice. Pomegranate juice is tart and piquant; superb for giving a sauce or dressing a little lift. Toss some of the seeds into a fresh fruit salad or even a green salad – any seeds that you don't need to use right away can be frozen successfully.

Lemon curd

You can never beat a jar of homemade lemon curd, smooth and buttery and zesty. The secret is never to let it boil!

- 500 g sugar
- juice of 6 ripe lemons
- finely grated zest of 6 ripe lemons
- 150 g unsalted butter
- 5 free-range eggs

Place the sugar, lemon juice and zest into a saucepan; heat gently and keep stirring until you have dissolved the sugar.

Once the sugar has dissolved, add the butter and melt it in the sugar and lemon mixture. Pour the mixture into the top of a double boiler; the water must be barely simmering.

Beat the eggs and run them through a sieve to remove any solids. Place the beaten eggs into a jug and then while you stir the lemon juice, slowly add the egg a tiny bit at a time. Keep stirring and cook gently for 25 to 30 minutes – never let it boil! The mixture should coat the back of a spoon when it is ready.

Pour into warm, sterilised jars and store in the fridge.

My favourite way to serve lemon curd is on warm toast, or as a quick dessert in buttery shortcrust pastry cups topped with a spoonful of mascarpone.

MAKES 3 x 250 ml JARS

Index